CONFEDERATION OF TOURISM AND HOSPITALITY

Housekeeping and Accommodation Operations

Study Guide

THIS STUDY GUIDE

BPP Learning Media is the **official publisher** for the CTH Diplomas in Hotel Management and Tourism Management.

IN THIS JULY 2009 FIRST EDITION

- The CTH 2009 syllabus, cross-referenced to the chapters
- Comprehensive syllabus coverage, reviewed and approved by CTH
- Plenty of activities, examples and discussion topics to demonstrate and practise technique
- Full index
- A full CTH past exam for exam practice

First edition July 2009

ISBN 9780 7517 7796 3

British Library Cataloguing-in-Publication Data
A catalogue record for this book
is available from the British Library

Published by

BPP Learning Media Ltd
BPP House, Aldine Place
London W12 8AA

www.bpp.com/learningmedia

Printed in the United Kingdom

Your learning materials, published by BPP Learning Media Ltd, are printed on paper sourced from sustainable, managed forests.

We are grateful to the Confederation of Tourism and Hospitality for permission to reproduce the syllabus and past examination questions and answers.

We would like to acknowledge the invaluable contribution of Andrew Pennington in the preparation of this Study Guide.

CONTENTS

How to use this Study Guide

This is the first edition of BPP Learning Media's ground-breaking Study Guide for the *Housekeeping and Accommodation Operations* paper of the CTH Diploma in Hotel Management. It has been specifically written to cover the syllabus, and has been fully reviewed by CTH.

To pass the examination you need a thorough understanding in all areas covered by the syllabus.

Recommended approach

(a)   To pass you need to be able to answer questions on **everything** specified by the syllabus. Read the Study Guide very carefully and do not skip any of it.

(b)   Learning is an **active** process. Do **all** the activities as you work through the Study Guide so you can be sure you really understand what you have read.

(c)   After you have covered the material in the Study Guide, work through the questions in the practice exam at the back.

(d)   Before you take the real exam, check that you still remember the material using the following quick revision plan.

   (i)   Read through the chapter learning objectives. Are there any gaps in your knowledge? If so, study the section again.

   (ii)   Read and learn the key terms.

   (iii)   Read and try to memorise the summary at the end of each chapter.

   (iv)   Do the self-test questions again. If you know what you're doing, they shouldn't take long.

This approach is only a suggestion. You or your college may well adapt it to suit your needs.

Remember this is a **practical** course.

(a)   Try to relate the material to your experience in the workplace or any other work experience you may have had.

(b)   Try to make as many links as you can to other CTH papers that you may be studying at the moment.

Help yourself study for your CTH exams

Exams for professional bodies such as CTH are very different from those you may have taken at school or college. You will be under **greater time pressure** before the exam – as you may be combining your study with work. There are many different ways of learning and so the BPP Learning Media Study Guide offers you a number of different tools to help you through. Here are some hints and tips: they are not plucked out of the air, but **based on research and experience**. (You don't need to know that long-term memory is in the same part of the brain as emotions and feelings – but it's a fact anyway.)

The right approach

1   **The right attitude**

   Believe in yourself

   Yes, there is a lot to learn. Yes, it is a challenge. But thousands have succeeded before and you can too.

   Remember why you're doing it

   Studying might seem a grind at times, but you are doing it for a reason: to advance your career.

2 **The right focus**

Read through the syllabus and the chapter objectives

These tell you what you are expected to know.

Study the Exam Paper section

It helps to be familiar with the structure of the exam that you are going to take.

3 **The right method**

The whole picture

You need to grasp the detail – but keeping in mind how everything fits into the whole picture will help you understand better.

- The **objectives and topic list** of each chapter put the material in context.
- The **syllabus content** shows you what you need to **grasp**.

In your own words

To absorb the information (and to practise your written communication skills), it helps to **put it into your own words**.

- **Take notes**
- Answer the **questions** in each chapter. You will practise your written communication skills, which become increasingly important as you progress through your CTH exams.
- Draw **mindmaps**. The chapter summaries can be a good starting point for this.
- Try **'teaching' a subject** to a colleague or friend.

Give yourself cues to jog your memory

The BPP Study Guide uses **bold** to **highlight key points**.

- Try **colour coding** with a highlighter pen.
- Write **key points** on cards.

4 **The right review**

Review, review, review

It is a **fact** that regularly reviewing a topic in summary form can **fix it in your memory**. Because **review** is so important, the BPP Study Guide helps you to do so in many ways.

- **Chapter summaries** draw together the key points in each chapter. Use them to recap each study session.
- The **self-test questions** are another review technique you can use to ensure that you have grasped the essentials.
- Go through the **examples and illustrations** in each chapter a second or third time.

Developing your personal study plan

BPP's **Learning to Learn Accountancy** book (which can be successfully used by students studying for any professional qualification) emphasises the need to prepare (and use) a study plan. Planning and sticking to the plan are key elements of learning success.

There are four steps you should work through.

STEP 1   **How do you learn?**

First you need to be aware of your style of learning. The BPP Learning Media **Learning to Learn Accountancy** book commits a chapter to this **self-discovery**. What types of intelligence do you display when learning? You might be advised to brush up on certain study skills before launching into this Study Guide.

BPP Learning Media's **Learning to Learn Accountancy** book helps you to identify what intelligences you show more strongly and then details how you can tailor your study process to your preferences. It also includes handy hints on how to develop intelligences you exhibit less strongly, but which might be needed as you study for your professional qualification.

Are you a **theorist** or are you more **practical**? If you would rather get to grips with a theory before trying to apply it in practice, you should follow the study sequence on page vii. If the reverse is true (you like to know why you are learning theory before you do so), you might be advised to flick through Study Guide chapters and look at examples, case studies and questions (Steps 8, 9 and 10 in the **suggested study sequence**) before reading through the detailed theory.

STEP 2   **How much time do you have?**

Work out the time you have available per week, given the following.

- The standard you have set yourself
- The time you need to set aside later for revision work
- The other exam(s) you are sitting
- Very importantly, practical matters such as work, travel, exercise, sleep and social life

Hours

Note your time available each week in box A.   A   [   ]

STEP 3   **Allocate your time**

- Take the time you have available per week for this Study Guide shown in box A, multiply it by the number of weeks available and insert the result in box B.   B   [   ]

- Divide the figure in box B by the number of chapters in this text and insert the result in box C.   C   [   ]

Remember that this is only a rough guide. Some of the chapters in this book are longer and more complicated than others, and you will find some subjects easier to understand than others.

STEP 4   **Implement**

Set about studying each chapter in the time shown in box C, following the key study steps in the order suggested by your particular learning style.

This is your personal **study plan**. You should try and combine it with the study sequence outlined below. You may want to modify the sequence a little (as has been suggested above) to adapt it to your **personal style**.

BPP Learning Media's **Learning to Learn Accountancy** gives further guidance on developing a study plan, and deciding where and when to study.

Suggested study sequence

It is likely that the best way to approach this Study Guide is to tackle the chapters in the order in which you find them. Taking into account your individual learning style, you could follow this sequence.

Key study steps	Activity
Step 1 **Topic list**	Look at the topic list at the start of each chapter. Each topic represents a section in the chapter.
Step 2 **Explanations**	Proceed methodically through the chapter, reading each section thoroughly and making sure you understand.
Step 3 **Definitions**	Definitions can often earn you **easy marks** if you state them clearly and correctly in an appropriate exam answer
Step 4 **Note taking**	Take brief notes, if you wish. Avoid the temptation to copy out too much. Remember that being able to put something into your own words is a sign of being able to understand it. If you find you cannot explain something you have read, read it again before you make the notes.
Step 5 **Examples**	Follow each through to its solution very carefully.
Step 6 **Discussion topics**	Study each one, and try to add flesh to them from your own experience. They are designed to show how the topics you are studying come alive (and often come unstuck) in the real world.
Step 7 **Activities**	Make a very good attempt at each one.
Step 8 **Answers**	Check yours against ours, and make sure you understand any discrepancies.
Step 9 **Chapter summary**	Work through it carefully, to make sure you have grasped the significance of all the key areas.
Step 10 **Self-test questions**	When you are happy that you have covered the chapter, use the self-test questions to check how much you have remembered of the topics covered and to practise questions in a variety of formats.
Step 11 **Question practice**	Either at this point, or later when you are thinking about revising, make a full attempt at the practice exam.

Moving on...

However you study, when you are ready to start your revision, you should still refer back to this Study Guide, both as a source of **reference** (you should find the index particularly helpful for this) and as a way to **review** (the chapter summaries and self-test questions help you here).

And remember to keep careful hold of this Study Guide – you will find it invaluable in your work.

> More advice on study skills can be found in BPP Learning Media's **Learning to Learn Accountancy book**.

Syllabus

DIPLOMA IN HOTEL MANAGEMENT MODULE SYLLABUS

DHM 132: Housekeeping and Accommodation Operations

Description

This module introduces students to the systems and procedures required for Housekeeping and Accommodation Operations. It provides an overview of the functions and supervisory aspects of the housekeeping and accommodation department. Students will develop knowledge and skills in departmental procedures as well as an understanding of safety and security responsibilities.

Summary of Learning Outcomes

To succeed in this module, students must;

- Demonstrate knowledge of the functional areas of the housekeeping and accommodation department

- Describe the operational and supervisory aspects of running an accommodation operation

- Investigate the purchase and range of furnishings available

- Examine the range of accommodation provided and the regular processes of cleaning and maintenance necessary to ensure the facilities and accommodation meets the customer requirements

- Identify common cleaning supplies and equipment used in the housekeeping department

- Describe the key features of the linen and laundry departments

- Describe the main responsibilities of the housekeeping department for the hotel's leisure facilities

- Explain the importance of security and safety within the housekeeping and accommodation department

- Explore measures to improve the environmental responsibilities of the hotel

Syllabus		Chapter
Introduction to housekeeping and accommodation operations	The organisation structure of the housekeeping and accommodation department.	
	Roles and responsibilities of managers, supervisors and staff.	
	The range of accommodation available in the commercial sector; hotels, motels, country house hotels.	1
	Liaison with other departments.	
Operational planning and procedures	The organisation and procedures involved in the cleaning of accommodation and public areas.	
	Allocation of work.	
	Standard operating procedures.	
	Routine methods of work.	2
	Main duties and tasks.	
	Standards and quality.	
	Pests and waste disposal.	

Furniture, fixtures and fabric	Flooring, carpets, wall coverings.	3
	Furniture and soft furnishings.	
	Beds and bedding.	
	Bathroom fitments and accessories.	
	The purchasing of capital expenditure items.	
	The use and care of hard and soft furnishings.	
Housekeeping equipment and supplies	Manual and mechanical cleaning equipment.	2
	Cleaning materials and their safe use and storage.	
	The purchasing of cleaning materials and supplies.	
Linen room and laundry facilities	Linen purchase and contract linen hire.	5
	Inspection, control and storage of linen.	
	Processes for dirty linen.	
	The work of the linen room.	
	The stocktaking of linen.	
	In-house and commercial laundries.	
Maintenance	Maintaining the overall appearance and working order of the hotel including guest rooms, public areas, common areas and the exterior of the building.	6
	Completing maintenance requests.	
	Conducting regular safety inspections and training staff on safety and emergency procedures.	
Leisure facilities	Care and maintenance of hotel leisure facilities.	4
	Maintaining health and safety in a leisure facility.	
Security and safety responsibilities	Prevention of accidents.	4
	Adhering to fire safety precautions.	
	Responsibilities in case of discovering a fire.	
	Safe working practices.	
	Security of guest rooms.	
	Risk management.	
	The procedures to be followed in the case of an emergency.	
	Legal responsibilities and requirements.	
Energy and environmental management	Recycling.	2, 4, 5
	Hazardous waste disposal.	
	Reducing energy consumption.	
	Minimising environmental impact	

Assessment

This module will be assessed via a 2½ hour examination, set and marked by CTH. The examination will cover the whole of the assessment criteria in this unit and will take the form of 10 x 2 mark questions and 5 x 4 mark questions in section A (40 marks). Section B will comprise of 5 x 20 mark questions of which candidates must select and answer three (60 marks). CTH is a London based awarding body and the syllabus content will in general reflect this. Any legislation and codes of practice will reflect the international nature of the industry and will not be country specific. International centres may find it advantageous to add local legislation or practice to their teaching but they should be aware that the CTH examination will not assess this local knowledge.

Further guidance

Recommended contact hours: 45   **Credits: 10**

Delivery Strategies

This module covers the theory of Housekeeping and Accommodation Operations, wherever possible this should be related to practical situations to reflect the nature of the commercial work environs.

Recommended Prior Learning

There is no required prior learning however students must have completed formal education to 18 years old or equivalent and an interest in Housekeeping and Accommodation Operations is essential.

Resources

It is strongly recommended that visits to organisations within the hospitality industry are undertaken to experience housekeeping and accommodation operations first hand. It is also highly desirable to organise a programme of guest speakers to add currency and vocational relevance. Learners need access to library and research facilities which should include some or all of the following:

Key text

Housekeeping and Accommodation Operations CTH Study Guide (2009), BPP Learning Media.

ISBN 9780 7517 7796 3

Supporting texts

- Branson & Lennox (1988), *Hotel, Hostel and Hospital Housekeeping* (5th edition), Hodder and Stoughton ISBN 0 7131 7732 2

- Jones, TJA (2007), *Professional Management of Housekeeping Operations*, (5th edition), John Wiley & Sons, Inc., ISBN 978-0-471-76244-7

- Kirk, D (1995), *Environmental Management for Hotels: A Student Handbook*, Butterworth Heinneman.

Magazines, Journals and other Publications

- Caterer and Hotelkeeper
- Hospitality

Websites:

www.bifm.org.uk	British Institute of Facilities Management
www.caterer.com	Caterer and Hotelkeeper
www.etsu.com	Energy Efficiency Enquiries Bureau
www.instituteofhospitality.org	Institute of Hospitality

Notes on recommended texts

This module should be based on the syllabus and the supporting BPP Learning Media CTH Study Guide.

The lecturer's lesson plans should be based on the module syllabus and supported by the BPP Learning Media CTH Study Guide for the subject. Lecturers may also use other relevant texts and supplementary material familiar to the lecturer and based on the lecturer's experience. It is not essential to use all the recommended texts and lecturers should use their experience to decide which ones are most appropriate for their students. Where available and appropriate, past module examinations are available to support lecturers.

CTH will always answer any questions from the centre's Head of Department either by e-mail or by phone.

The exam paper

All the CTH examinations for the Diploma in Hotel Management and Diploma in Tourism Management follow the same format.

Exam duration: 2½ hours

Section A: Marks

Ten	2 mark questions	20
Five	4 mark questions	20
		40

All questions in Section A are compulsory

Section B:

Five	20-mark questions (candidates must choose three)	60
		100

Other titles in this series

BPP Learning Media publishes the following titles for the CTH Diploma in Hotel Management

- Food and Beverage Operations
- Food Hygiene, Health and Safety
- Front Office Operations
- Housekeeping and Accommodation Operations
- Finance for Tourism and Hospitality*
- Introduction to Business Operations*
- Marketing*
- The Tourism Industry*
- The Global Hospitality Industry

*These titles are also papers within the CTH Diploma in Tourism Management qualification.

In July 2010 BPP Learning Media will publish the remaining titles for the Diploma in Tourism Management:

- Travel Geography
- Travel Agency and Tour Guide Operations
- Introduction to Tourism Economics
- Special Interest Tourism
- Destination Analysis

CHAPTER 1

INTRODUCTION TO HOUSEKEEPING

Chapter objectives

By the end of this chapter you will be able to

- Explain the importance of good housekeeping for customers, employees and the organisation
- Present strategies for effective housekeeping quality control
- Discuss key positions within the department, their responsibilities and organisation
- Describe the housekeeping departments relationship with other departments within the hotel

Topic list
Introduction to housekeeping
Organisation, staffing and structures
Liaison with other departments

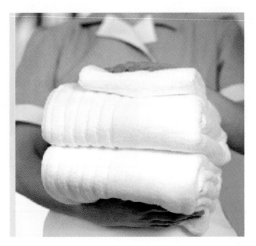

Source: http://www.cambridgesuiteshalifax.com

1 Introduction to housekeeping

"Efficiently managed housekeeping departments ensure the cleanliness, maintenance, and aesthetic appeal of lodging properties. The housekeeping department not only prepares clean guest rooms on a timely basis for arriving guests, it also cleans and maintains everything in the hotel."

Kappa, Nitschke and Schappert (1997)

"Housekeeping is the customer's **first** impression and **last** impression."

ACTIVITY 1   30 minutes

Have you ever had a negative housekeeping experience? Maybe you have stayed the night in a hotel bedroom that was not up to standard or have dined in a restaurant with poor cleanliness. How did you feel? Complete a mind map detailing your emotions, feelings, thoughts, reasons and solutions.

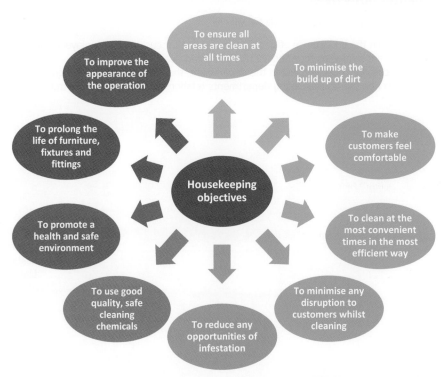

Figure 1.1: Housekeeping objectives

Challenges for the Housekeeping department.

- Responsibility for the largest volume of area within the hotel
- The largest department in the hotel
- In most cases, has the largest departmental staff count in the hotel
- Hard to attract skilled employees
- Hard to retain employees
- Hard to motivate employees

Good housekeeping	Poor housekeeping
Customers feel comfortable	Customers feel uncomfortable
Customers are satisfied	Customers are unsatisfied
Praise and gratuities	Complaints and discounts
Customers return	Customers switch to other hotels
Good word of mouth	Negative word of mouth
Employees are satisfied	Employees are unhappy
Employees are retained	Employees leave

The importance of high standards of cleanliness to the guest cannot be underestimated. We have discussed the issue of positive first impressions – it is estimated that guests form impressions in seconds and these impressions last.

- A guest that arrives at the hotel and enters through a lobby where the ashtrays are full, the furniture in disarray and the flowers wilting, will have formed negative impressions before they even check-in.

- Positive first impressions can be undermined when guests arrive in a room that has not been adequately prepared or maintained. Dirty restaurants can impair the most delicious meal experience.

- The Housekeeping management aims to deliver high standards in generally challenging conditions, working with limited resources in a pressurised environment.

FOR DISCUSSION

Discuss which of the following is the most important reason for a guest selecting and returning to a hotel.

- Good service
- Cleanliness
- Facilities
- Price
- Good products

Quality controls in Housekeeping

Figure 1.2: Key ways to provide good housekeeping

2 Organisation, staffing and structures

2.1 The Executive Housekeeper

The executive housekeeper within the hotel organisation is one of the main managers within any large hotel.

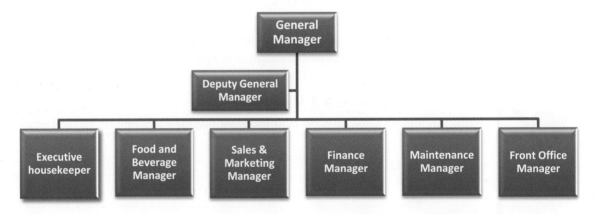

Figure 1.3: Hotel department managers

The executive housekeeper or (housekeeping manager) is normally a high level position within the hotel holding much responsibility, as outlined in the job description, below.

Job Description

Job title: Head Housekeeper

Responsible to: Assistant General Manager

Main duties

- To comply with all statutory and company regulations relating to the health & safety, hygiene, conduct of employees, fire emergency procedures, security of premises and of property.

- To be responsible for the cleanliness of all public areas, bedrooms and offices.

- To have responsibility for the supervision, training and development of the Housekeeping team.

- To ensure the smooth operation of the Linen Room within the hotel.

- To manage the compilation of weekly wage sheets and to hand them over to the Personnel department by 10.00 am each Monday.

- To liaise closely with the Personnel department with regard to recruitment and disciplinary matters.

- To ensure the correct training and retraining of all staff to sustain company standards of cleanliness.

- To liaise on a regular basis with the Maintenance department with regard to room maintenance.

- To maintain correct staffing levels in accordance with company business.

- To be responsible for the purchase of all cleaning materials and maintaining adequate stocks while controlling expenditure in line with company budget.

- To be aware of, and be responsible for, all contract cleaning, including carpets, windows.

- To maintain a high level of communication between the Housekeeping and Reception departments to ensure the least inconvenience to guests.

- To maintain a high level of quality control in all areas through room checks and correct delegation to supervisors and room attendants.

- To maintain all Housekeeping storerooms in an orderly and tidy manner.

- To comply with COSHH regulations and to ensure that staff adhere to these regulations.

- To comply with company image standards.

Miscellaneous

- To act in accordance with fire instructions.

- To observe all security, health & safety regulations.

- To ensure that any hazard is immediately reported to the Head of Department or Duty Manager.

- To maintain the highest standards of hygiene and cleanliness in all aspects of your work.

- To undertake any other duty which you may be reasonably requested to do in carrying out your job.

As an executive manager the housekeeper is required to carry out various managerial functions as shown below.

Figure 1.4: Head housekeeper's managerial functions

ACTIVITY 2   4 5   m i n u t e s

For each of the seven management functions detailed above, what would an executive housekeeper do for each task? For example in planning, an executive housekeeper would plan employee training, meetings and checks.

2.2 The Housekeeping team

Personal attributes of Housekeeping staff:

Adapted from *Raghubalan and Raghubalan (2007)*

Staffing within the organisation would vary depending on:

- Size of operation and area to be cleaned
- Quantity of rooms
- Standard of hotel
- Amount of facilities in the hotel
- Availability of skilled labour
- Housekeeping labour budget

The following table presents the typical housekeeping structures and services available in different hospitality operations.

	Employee organisation and structure	Housekeeping services offered
Bed and Breakfast	Owner carries out most cleaning. May employ part-time staff to assist when busy. Linen may also be cleaned in-house	▪ General room cleaning during occupancy and on departure ▪ Cleaning of entrance and public areas
Budget Hotel	As rooms are the main product for budget hotels the hotel would in most cases employ an individual to manage the room cleaning. Room attendants may be outsourced to minimise costs and keep in line with main mission of hotel. Linen outsourced	▪ General room cleaning during occupancy and on departure ▪ Cleaning of entrance and public areas, bar and restaurant
4-Star Hotel **Holiday Inn**	Refer to Figure 1.5 below.	▪ Room cleaning ▪ Turndown service ▪ Special amenities in room
5-Star Hotel	Similar structure to 4-star but staffing ratios would be higher due to service quality.	▪ Similar to 4-star but more deluxe ▪ Less likely to outsource room cleaning ▪ Longer room cleaning times ▪ Greater quantity of customers to receive in-room amenities ▪ Better quality linen, furniture and design ▪ Butler and valet service ▪ Own florist

DEFINITION

Turndown Service – this is a service normally carried out around 6.00 pm when a chambermaid or evening maid enters an occupied room and:

- ▪ Closes curtains or drapes
- ▪ Dims lights
- ▪ Folds down bed top sheet
- ▪ Replenishes towels, toiletries and stationery
- ▪ Places room service breakfast menu on guest's pillow
- ▪ Places a complimentary mint or chocolate on the pillow or bottled water at the bedside
- ▪ Places disposable slippers beside the bed
- ▪ Empties rubbish bins

DEFINITION

Amenities are 'complimentary' (free of charge) items that would be delivered to regular, VIP, returning and complaint guests.

Amenities include items such as:

- Fruit basket
- Cheese board
- Bottle of wine or champagne
- Chocolates
- Fresh flowers

Amenities are normally commissioned by the guest relations or sales executive and delivered to the room by the Room Service department.

The chart on the following page illustrates a typical housekeeping operation for a 4-star hotel followed by an outline of the key positions required to staff the department together with their respective roles and responsibilities.

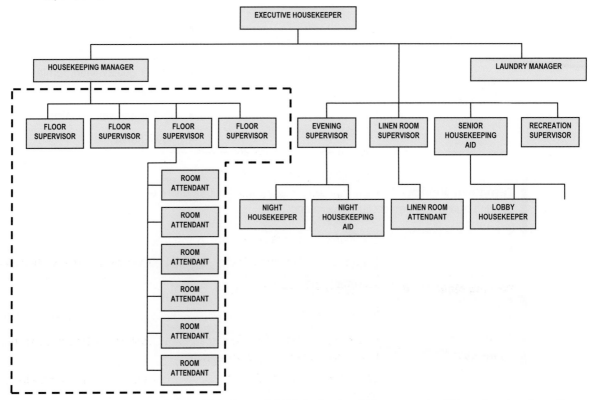

Source: Thomas J.A. Jones (2008) Professional Management of Housekeeping Operations

Figure 1.5: Housekeeping organisational chart for a 4-star hotel

Key Positions	Responsibilities
Deputy Executive Housekeeper (or Floor Housekeeper, depending on size and organisation of hotel)	▪ Deputises for Executive Housekeeper ▪ To quality-check rooms ▪ Checks rooms prior to arrival, during occupancy and after departure ▪ Releases clean rooms to reception ▪ Coaches room attendants ▪ Periodic training of employees ▪ Conducts shift briefings ▪ Maintain the highest standards of rooms and suites of their floors ▪ Organise and schedule rooms and suites maintenance for example spring clean, wall cleaning and ceiling washing, high dusting and under-bed vacuuming ▪ Organise room attendants to service and clean the room or suites which are under priority ▪ Organise all cleaning chemicals and equipment for their floor each day ▪ Check rooms and suites which are due out on the day ▪ Prepare any relevant paperwork for the next day ▪ Hand over the shift and all information regarding their floor to the evening housekeepers ▪ Communicate any issues regarding rooms and suites with the housekeeping office co-ordinator and senior housekeepers ▪ Organise floor maid service areas ▪ Carry out weekly and monthly stock-take ▪ Check and control room and bathroom amenities stock ▪ Accommodate guest needs and expectations on a daily basis
Room Attendant (or chambermaid)	▪ Attend daily briefings ▪ Stock service trolleys ▪ Clean rooms and suites to the highest standards ▪ Vacuum and dust rooms and suites ▪ Maintain maid service pantry areas ▪ Communicate with customers ▪ Attend training sessions ▪ Communicate with floor housekeeper ▪ Report any broken and missing items in rooms and suites to floor housekeeper
Evening Maid	▪ Completes 'turn down' service ▪ Deals with customers' requests
Public Area Supervisor	▪ Check and inspect the public areas such as front hall, ballroom, public rest rooms and cloakrooms, stair cases, etc ▪ Check and inspect the function rooms and meeting rooms with private event's team ▪ Check and inspect staff changing rooms and restrooms

	▪ Maintain the highest standards of public areas and staff areas
	▪ Organise public area attendants working rota
	▪ Communicate any issue and challenge with the public areas cleaner contactors
	▪ Conducts weekly and monthly stock-takes
Public Area Cleaner (PA)	▪ Clean public areas to include (lobby, lifts, corridors, public toilets, offices and service areas)
	▪ Report any faults or defects
	▪ Communicate with customers
	▪ Make public areas clean and well presented
	▪ (The cleaning of areas such as restaurants and bars are normally partly cleaned by the outlet staff and partly by public area staff)
Housekeeping Porter	▪ Communicate with floor housekeepers
	▪ Assist with rooms and suites maintenance as and when required
	▪ Help floor housekeepers with the weekly and monthly stock-take
	▪ Remove and empty the rubbish bins from the maid service areas
	▪ Refill all cleaning chemicals at the end of the shift
	▪ Assist with floor housekeepers' and room attendants' requests
	▪ Maintain cleanliness and tidiness of maid service areas
	▪ Move furniture as per floor housekeepers' instructions
	▪ Organise and maintain the storage and bed and linen cupboards
	▪ Restock floor linen room pantry for room attendants
	▪ Deliver and collect 'Special Request' to rooms (cots, blankets, extra towels)
	▪ Transport dirty laundry to linen room from floors
	▪ Assist room attendants during peak times
	▪ Assist room attendants with deep cleaning activities
Valet	▪ Wash and iron guest laundry items
	▪ Send and arrange return of guest dry-cleaning items
	▪ Carry out minor guest repairs on customers' laundry
	▪ Shoe cleaning
	▪ Pressing services
	▪ Charge to guest account folio for guest laundry items
	▪ Do weekly and monthly stock-take for the valet
	▪ Communicate any issues regarding rooms and suites with housekeeping office co-ordinator and senior housekeepers
	▪ Organise any guest belongings and lost property items to and from storage
	(Note this position should not be confused with Valet Parkers that in some hotels park cars for customers.)
Linen Room Attendant	▪ Send out and receive all staff laundry and dry-cleaning items on a daily basis
	▪ Do weekly and monthly stock-takes for the linen room
	▪ Organise staff laundry and dry-cleaning of uniforms
	▪ Carry out linen repairs

	<ul><li>Deliver all linen to the maid service (Pantry) on each floor as per stock levels</li><li>Communicate with the linen and laundry room manager and the floor housekeepers</li><li>Communicate any issues regarding linen room with housekeeping office co-ordinator and senior housekeepers</li></ul>
Laundry Attendants	<ul><li>Wash and iron in-house laundry items</li><li>Send and receive in-house dry-cleaning items to departments or external laundry</li><li>Separate all types of linen and laundry items before the items are processed</li><li>Fold all types of linen and laundry items before delivery back to the floors</li><li>Communicate with the linen and laundry room manager and the floor housekeepers</li></ul>
Butler (This position is normally only found in very high quality hotels)	For housekeeping duties only.<ul><li>Unpack and pack guest belongings</li><li>Send and receive guest laundry and dry-cleaning items from the valet</li><li>Communicate any issues regarding rooms and suites with housekeeping office co-ordinator and senior housekeepers</li><li>Maintain the highest standards of guest rooms and suites</li><li>Report any broken and missing items in feature suites to the floor housekeepers</li></ul>
Linen Porter	<ul><li>Assists with transporting soiled linen from rooms to linen room</li><li>Assists with replenishing of fresh linen to floor pantries</li><li>Delivers additional fresh linen to customers on request</li><li>Collects and delivers customers' dry-cleaning to and from rooms</li></ul>
Night Contract Cleaning	Specialist companies are also used for cleaning duties at night time. This can include general vacuuming of public areas and also more specialised cleaning such as polishing of marble floors within the lobby. Night cleaning is necessary as the cleaning of public areas in depth can be difficult during the day time due to customers being present in the hotel. Night cleaning can be in-depth and with minimal noise disturbance to customers.

Note

Agency personnel. Many hotels use agency housekeeping personnel in addition to their full-time staff during times of high demand or to cover employee holidays or sick days.

DEFINITION

Floor Pantry – in most hotels, each floor would have a pantry used for storage of linen, chemicals and cleaning resources.

DEFINITION

Special Requests – Items that may be requested by customers in addition to the normal services provided. This may include:

- Roll away beds
- Cots
- Extra pillows, blankets or towels
- Ironing boards
- International mains adaptors
- Emergency grooming kits – for example, toothpaste and shaver

2.3 Room attendants

Source: http://www.butlerforyou

Room attendant is one of the most common positions and makes up the majority of the workforce in a hotel.

ACTIVITY 3   10 minutes

Some of the challenges faced by a room attendant could potentially lead to a high rate of employee turnover. As an executive housekeeper, complete the following table and give ways that you could overcome some of these problems.

Challenges of the job	Solutions?
Work is physical (lifting, carrying) and can be tiring	
Work can be lonely	
Work can be messy and demotivating	
Work can be dangerous (chemicals, needles, slipping)	

Opportunities

- New skills
- Sociable hours
- Independent work
- Tips
- Fast progression for right individuals

Outsourcing room cleaning

Trend: Many hotels now outsource their room cleaning to an external cleaning company as shown in the following diagram. However, as the table below illustrates, there are positive and negative attributes.

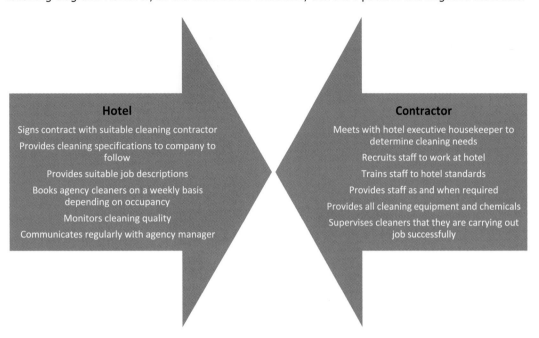

Hotel

Signs contract with suitable cleaning contractor

Provides cleaning specifications to company to follow

Provides suitable job descriptions

Books agency cleaners on a weekly basis depending on occupancy

Monitors cleaning quality

Communicates regularly with agency manager

Contractor

Meets with hotel executive housekeeper to determine cleaning needs

Recruits staff to work at hotel

Trains staff to hotel standards

Provides staff as and when required

Provides all cleaning equipment and chemicals

Supervises cleaners that they are carrying out job successfully

Figure 1.6: Outsourcing housekeeping

Opportunities for hotel	Challenges for hotel
▪ Reduced expenditure overall (recruitment, training, turnover)	▪ Potential loss of control
▪ More accurate labour forecasting, deployment and utilisation	▪ Different work teams within hotel
▪ Specialisation	▪ Casual staff may not be familiar with loyal customers
▪ Able to focus on other activities	

A C T I V I T Y   4   **3 0   m i n u t e s**

As executive housekeeper detail how you would overcome the challenges as listed in the above table.

3 Liaison with other departments

Housekeeping is a support department and works closely with many departments within the hotel.

It is also commonly the case that 'daily' agency maids are employed by hotels to cope with the fluctuations of room occupancy.

Figure 1.7: Housekeeping communication hub

3.1 Communication: Housekeeping and Front Office

Good **teamwork** between these two departments is essential to daily hotel operations. The primary communication from the Housekeeping department is with Front Office desk staff.

Each night, a front desk agent produces an **occupancy report** which lists rooms occupied that night and indicates guests who are expected to check-out the following day. The early housekeeper picks up this list early the next morning and schedules the occupied rooms for cleaning. As guests check-out, the Front Desk notifies Housekeeping, which ensures that these rooms are given top priority so that clean rooms are available for arriving guests.

At the end of the shift, the Housekeeping department prepares a **housekeeping status report**, as shown below, based on physical check of each room. This report indicates the current housekeeping status of each room and is compared with the front office occupancy report, and any discrepancies brought to the attention of the front office manager. A **room status discrepancy** is a situation in which the housekeeping department's description of a room status differs from the room status information being used by the Front Desk to assign guestrooms. *Adapted from Kappa et al. (1997)*

		Status
Room 212	Mr White	DND
Room 213	Mrs Tsang	Due out
Room 214	Mr and Mrs Jones	Occupied
Room 215	Mr Edwards	Occupied
Room 216	Mr Nakamura	Due out
Room 217	Mr Patel	Due out

Room status terminology

Occupied	A guest is currently registered to the room
Complimentary	The room is occupied, but the guest is assessed no charge for its use
Stayover	The guest is not checking-out today and will remain at least one more night
On-change (or vacant dirty)	The guest has departed, but the room has not yet been cleaned and readied for resale
Do not disturb (DND)	The guest has requested not to be disturbed
Sleep-out	A guest is registered to the room, but the bed has not been used
Skipper	The guest has left the hotel without making arrangements to settle his/her account
Sleeper	The guest has settled his/her account and left the hotel, but the front office staff have failed to properly update the room's status from occupied
Vacant and ready (or vacant, clean and inspected)	The room has been cleaned and inspected and is ready for an arriving guest
Out-of-order (OOO)	The room cannot be assigned to the guest. A room may be out-of-order for a variety of reasons, including the need for maintenance, refurbishing, and extensive cleaning
Lock-out (or double locked)	The room has been locked so that the guest cannot re-enter until he/she is cleared by an hotel official
Did not check-out (DNCO)	The guest made arrangements to settle his or her account (and thus is not a skipper) but has left without informing the front office
Due out	The room is expected to become vacant after the following day's checkout time
Checked-out (or departed)	The guest has settled his or her account, returned the room keys, and left the hotel
Late check-out	The guest has requested and is being allowed to check out later than the hotel's standard check-out time

Source: Kappa et al. (1997)

The Front Office desk can use two types of system to track current room status: *Room rack* (manually) and *Room-status system* (computerised). Nowadays room attendants can enter a code on the room telephone and change the room status in the hotel's computer system. It is a fast procedure and avoids delays or errors in the system.

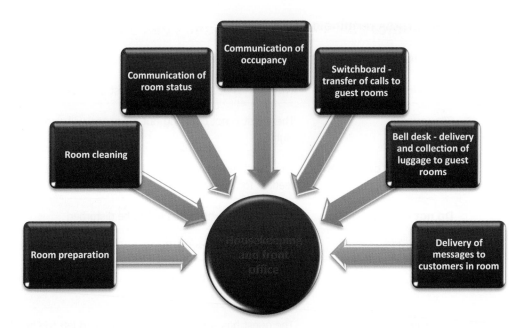

Bell desk – a bell desk consists of concierge, luggage and transportation hall and portering services.

DEFINITION

3.2 Communication: Housekeeping and Maintenance

The upkeep of the hotel is very important for avoiding any guest dissatisfaction. The communication between housekeeping and maintenance should be efficient and fast.

The maintenance of the hotel, therefore, depends on the responsibilities of Housekeeping to check daily all the equipment, furniture and fixtures and report any damage or problem to the Maintenance department.

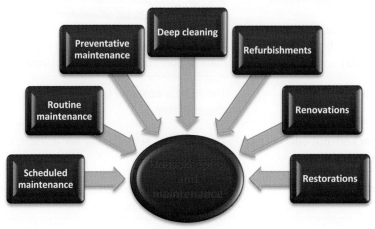

ACTIVITY 5   **1 5 m i n u t e s**

Research and detail the difference between:

- Room refurbishment
- Room renovation
- Room restoration

3.3 Communication: Housekeeping and Food and Beverage

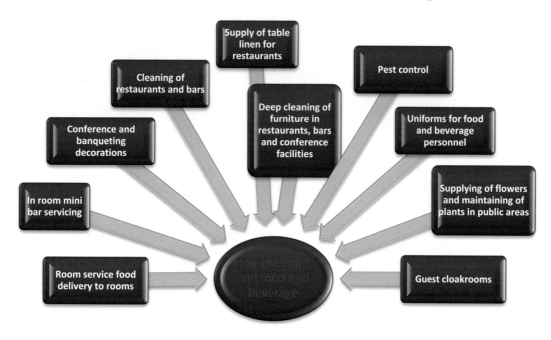

Note: Mini Bar servicing can, in some hotels, be carried out by the housekeeping department to reduce further disturbance to in-room guests.

3.4 Communication: Housekeeping and Administration

3.5   Communication: Housekeeping and Security

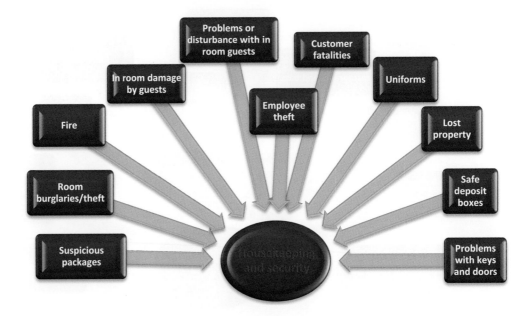

3.6   Communication: Housekeeping and Sales

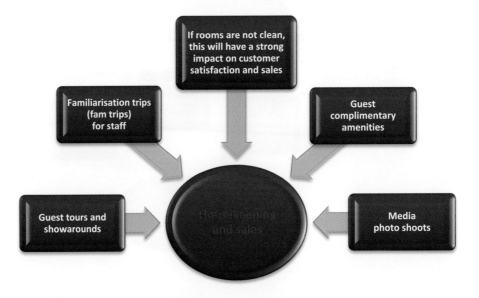

Familiarisation trips – when the Sales Department invites travel operators and other booking agents to visit and sample the hotel and its facilities. Housekeeping plays a vital role in these tours, ensuring that a good, clean impression is achieved.

DEFINITION

BPP)))
LEARNING MEDIA

3.7   Communication: Housekeeping and Leisure

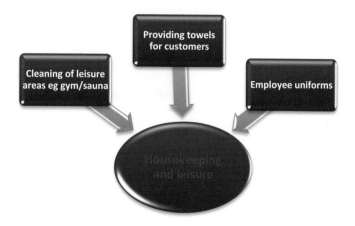

ACTIVITY 6   **3 0   m i n u t e s**

As executive housekeeper, what ten ways would you use to motivate your staff and your room attendants, in particular, to make the job more interesting?

SUMMARY

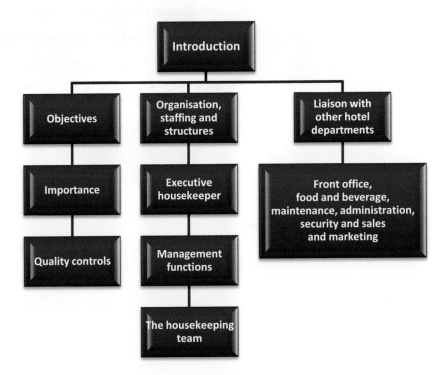

SELF-TEST QUESTIONS

1 Is Housekeeping the first or the last impression?

2 Name any three ways to achieve good housekeeping standards.

3 Would a turndown service take place in the morning, afternoon or evening?

4 Fresh flowers, chocolates or champagne provided to customers in rooms are examples of what?

5 Which employee is responsible for cleaning the lobby, lifts and public toilets?

6 Which employee is responsible for delivering guest requests to rooms?

7 Which type of hotel would not normally outsource its room cleaning?

8 A manual system for tracking guest room status is a..?

9 Which other department within a hotel has most communication with housekeeping?

10 What is meant by a hotel/room restoration?

SELF-TEST ANSWERS

1 Both

2 Any answer in Figure 1.2

3 The evening

4 Complimentary guest room amenities

5 A Public Area Cleaner

6 A Housekeeping Porter

7 A high quality hotel

8 A 'Room Rack'

9 Front Office/Reception

10 Restoring the facility to its original state

ANSWERS TO ACTIVITIES

1 A mind map is a diagram used to present thoughts, and ideas around a central topic or theme. Here is an example:

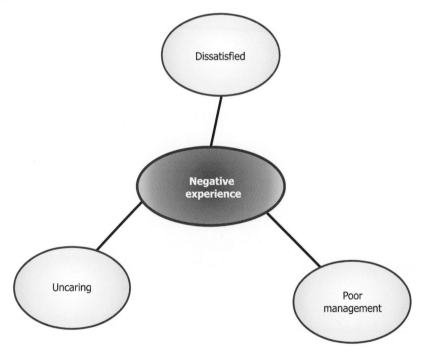

2

Planning	▪ Equipment Supplies ▪ Budgets ▪ Staffing
Organising	▪ Meetings ▪ Training ▪ Spot checks ▪ Inventories
Coordinating	▪ Manpower ▪ Casual Labour ▪ Cleaning tasks
Staffing	▪ Recruitment ▪ Interviews ▪ Training ▪ Incentives ▪ Motivating ▪ Evaluating ▪ Appraisals ▪ Discipline
Directing	▪ Contractors ▪ Employees ▪ Supervisors ▪ Management ▪ Customers
Controlling	▪ Labour Expenses ▪ Chemical expenses ▪ Standards
Evaluating	▪ Customer satisfaction ▪ Employee customer satisfaction ▪ Working methods ▪ Performance of resources

3

Challenges of the job	Solutions
Work is physical (lifting, carrying) and can be tiring	■ Effective manpower scheduling ■ Regular scheduled breaks ■ Manual handling training ■ Correct lifting techniques ■ Working in pairs when deep cleaning
Work can be lonely	Team cleaning – work is carried out in pairs to make work less lonely. Other advantages to team cleaning: time goes quicker, your partner can assist with any lifting, if accidents occur then someone is present to assist and employees are far less likely to call in sick if they feel they will let down their working partner.
Work can be messy and demotivating	■ Ensure customers behave correctly with a set of house rules ■ Supervisors need to provide full support to room cleanings when dealing with particularly messy rooms ■ Planned social events, employee of the month award and regular praise, instruction and training will make a hard job more worthwhile.
Work can be dangerous (chemicals, needles, slipping)	■ Health and Safety training for all employees ■ Refresher training ■ Clear standards for employees to follow enforced by efficient departmental supervision

4

Challenges for hotel	Solutions
Potential loss of control	■ Clear cleaning specifications for each cleaning task ■ Penalties enforced when specifications not followed by agency personnel ■ Regular performance meetings with management of contract company
Different work teams within hotel	■ Schedule training or social events to build team spirit
Casual staff may not be familiar with loyal customers	■ Photographs with names of regular and VIP customers ■ Casual staff to attend housekeeping briefings cleanings when dealing with particularly messy rooms ■ Planned social events, employee of the month award and regular praise, instruction and training will make a hard job more worthwhile

5 **Room refurbishment**

This is to decorate after the room has become tired following years of wear and tear. It is the least costly option and attempts to rejuvenate the room without too much expense. This would include repainting, wall papering, etc. This helps to maintain market share against newer competitors with more modern room facilities.

Room renovation

To renovate is to change the design of the room through decoration, structural amendments and furnishings. This would be conducted when target market or external consumer trends demand new features in room design.

Room restoration

To restore the room to its original condition. A lot of old properties will attempt to restore rooms to the original style of the time period of development.

6 **Could include**

- Team cleaning
- Planned social events
- Job chats
- Regular appraisals
- Ongoing training
- Regular praise
- Employee of the month schemes
- Incentives for good performance
- Job rotation
- Clear development and promotion schemes
- Empower maids to self check rooms
- Provide regular breaks
- Provide good, safe resources

CHAPTER 2

OPERATIONAL PLANNING

Chapter objectives

By the end of this chapter you will be able to

- Explain the importance of cleaning within hotels
- Outline the main steps in planning the cleaning of guest bedrooms
- Describe the purpose of a performance standard
- Plan the resources required to service accommodation
- Describe some of the factors that would need to be considered when planning cleaning
- Explain some of the roles in the accommodation services department

Source: http://www.delivery.superstock.com

Like all other managers in a hotel, the executive housekeeper uses available resources to attain objectives set up by top management executives. Resources include people, money, time, work methods, materials, energy and equipment. These resources are in limited supply, and most executive housekeepers will readily admit that they rarely have all the resources they would like. Therefore, an important part of the executive housekeeper's job is planning how to use these limited resorces available to attain the hotel's objectives.

Kappa et al. (1997)

1 Introduction

We will begin by investigating 'soiling', its definition, distribution and its removal.

DEFINITION

Soil/Dirt. This can be defined as an accumulation of dust and other foreign matter, such as stains and spillages, held together by moisture or grease.

1.1 Soil types

- **Organic (loose, dry)** – commonly referred to as dust. It can usually be removed with direct mechanical action, as long as it stays dry. It can be swept, dusted, mopped, wiped, vacuumed or wet mopped with little or no chemical action required. Any surface that has not been cleaned in 12 hours will have dust accumulated on it. The longer it remains on a surface, the better chance it has of becoming oily, sticky soil from contamination with other substances, even from moisture in the air or from air conditioning units.

- **Inorganic (oily, sticky)** – soil or dirt is almost always mixed with grease or other oily materials which make the dirt stick to a surface. The longer dirt remains on a surface, the more it tends to bond to the surface and the harder it is to remove.

Soil build-up can be prevented by:

- Reducing the opportunity for soil to enter the establishment
- Minimising the build-up of soil within the establishment (see theory of dirt, illustrated below)

The theory of dirt

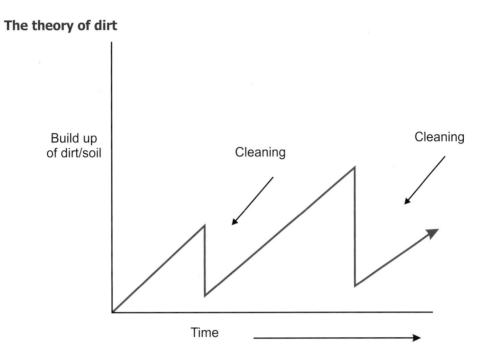

Soil is introduced into the workplace in many different ways, as shown in the following table.

Cause/ distribution	Examples		Solutions/prevention
Humans and employees	Poor hygiene	Poor handwashing	Signs, training, education, supervision, adaquate bathing/washing facilities
	Litter		Dustbins, signs
	Mistakes	Spillages	Training/prompt removal by cleaning
	Deliberate	Vandalism, graffitti	Code of conduct/rules
	Natural	Shredding skin, hair loss, perspiration	Personal grooming
	Disease (human contamination/virus)	Sneezing, coughing	
Employees	Bringing in soil from outside	Dirt on clothing	Changing rooms, standards, employee rules and regulations
Weather	Rain/snow	Water/sludge	Door mats/temporary entry carpets/umbrella holders/umbrella disposable bags
External matter/foliage	Leaves, earth, dust, litter, debris	Visitors/employees bring in on footwear	Entry mats, foot scrapers

Cause/ distribution	Examples		Solutions/prevention
Equipment	Machinery	Grease, dust, ventilation	Regular cleaning/cleaning schedules
Insects, vermin and pests	Cockroaches, rats, flies	Pests enter through the atmosphere, deliveries, luggage, cracks in maintenance, delivery areas, poor food hygiene, storage and disposal	Cover bins, keep door closed, thorough checks on delivery
The atmosphere	Smoke, exhausts, dust	The atmosphere deposits soil	Regular cleaning, good ventilation and extraction
Natural	Decay/deterioration	Interior and exterior – buildings, paintwork, stone	Regular maintenance

1.2   Cleaning agents

To assist in the removal of soil, a selection of chemicals are available, as given in the chart, below. When using cleaning agents one should remember to:

- Use the right chemical for the right job
- Always read the label
- Follow the cleaning specification
- Use the correct quantity
- Apply in the correct way
- Apply safely and with care

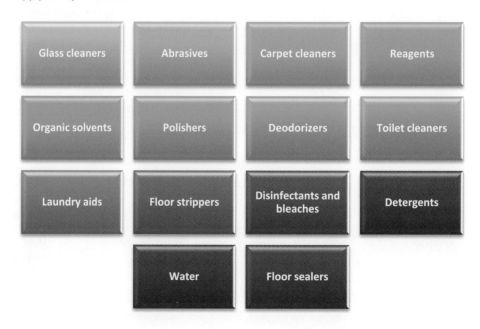

Source: Raghubalan and Raghubalan (2007)

1.3 Cleaning agents are applied using different methods

Figure 2.3: Cleaning methods

1.4 Cleaning equipment

Manual equipment	Mechanical equipment
▪ Brushes	▪ Vacuum cleaners
▪ Chamois leather	▪ Wet vacuums
▪ Dusters	▪ Wet extractors
▪ Dustpan and brush	▪ Rotary machines
▪ Mop and bucket	
▪ Ladders	
▪ Trolleys	
▪ Squeegee	
▪ Sprayers	

A C T I V I T Y   1   **4 5   m i n u t e s**

When would the equipment listed above be used?

1.5 Quality control in Housekeeping

To ensure that quality cleaning is achieved a combination of the following approaches are required.

- Effective leadership
- Standards of performance
- Effective human resources (recruitment, training and incentives)
- Quality sourcing
- Effective service recovery and complaint handling
- Quality schemes
- Quality feedback and monitoring systems
- Mystery visits

"To consistently meet or exceed customer expectations by providing products and services at prices that creates value for customers and profits for the company". *Woods and King, 2002*

2 Types of cleaning

1. **Daily** – rooms and public areas (this is the routine cleaning).
2. **Weekly** (cleaning tasks that are not required on a daily basis).
3. **Periodic/deep** cleaning (in-depth cleaning mostly carried out in *low season*).

2.1 Organisation of guest room cleaning

Raghubalan and Raghubalan (2007) explain the four main cleaning methods.

1. **Orthodox/conventional/traditional cleaning**. In this cleaning approach the employee completes all the tasks in one guest room before going on to the next room in the section allotted to him/her. On average, an employee may be required to clean 12-20 rooms in an eight-hour shift, not including break times.

FOR DISCUSSION

How many rooms per day is acceptable for one attendant to clean?

2. **Block cleaning**. The employee moves from room to room and completes the same task in every room, before returning to begin the cycle again for the next task on the list. This involves 'blocking' several rooms at a time to form a 'room section', and usually more than one employee will be at work in the section. For instance, one employee might make all the beds in that particular room section, while another employee cleans the toilets, and a third dusts and cleans the area, replenishing supplies.

3. **Team cleaning**. Two or more people work together in the same area, either on the same task or on different tasks. To organise the team cleaning of guest rooms, two employees may be scheduled to clean 30- 35 guest rooms a day.

Advantages	Disadvantages
Relationships formed between employees	Co-workers may talk which may disrupt work
Less likely to call in sick and let down cleaning partner	Partnerships may not always be compatible (personality conflicts)
Easier to lift heavy items when working in pairs	
Time passes faster due to having companionship	
If accidents were to occur, partner is on hand to assist	
Makes job more interesting and less lonely	

4.   **Deep cleaning**. Cleaning that is pre-scheduled, and in-depth. Examples include:

- Window cleaning
- Spring cleaning
- Turning mattresses
- Shampooing carpets
- Moving furniture
- Pest control
- Cleaning chandeliers

2.2   The principles of cleaning

- *Remove* all surface soil and obstructions before cleaning.
- Follow the *least obtrusive* and *non-disturbing* methods of cleaning, especially early in the morning.
- *Restore* all surfaces to as near perfect condition as soon as possible.
- Always use the *simplest method* of cleaning and the *mildest cleaning agent*.
- *Beware* of safety hazards.
- Remove all dust and dirt, *do not transfer* to another area.
- Carry out cleaning in the *quickest possible time*.

3   Guest room cleaning

No other feature or service provided will impress the guest more than a spotlessly clean and comfortable guestroom. The condition of the guest room conveys a critical message to guests. It shows the care that the property puts into creating a clean, safe, and pleasant environment for its guests. Housekeeping plays a greater role than any other department in ensuring that this product meets the standards that guests need and expect.   *Kappa et al. (1997)*

3.1   Planning room cleaning

When cleaning rooms it needs to be:

- Efficient
- Systematic
- Thorough
- Necessary
- Cost effective

When planning the cleaning of guest rooms the executive housekeeper breaks the tasks down into a set of systematic steps.

- *What* needs to be cleaned (inventory list)
- *When* it needs to be cleaned (frequency schedule)
- *How* it needs to be cleaned (performance and productivity standards)

Step 1

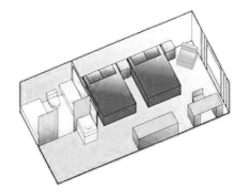

Using a room plan, a list is compiled of all furniture, fixtures and equipment in the room. This is sometimes referred to as an *'in-room inventory'*.

Furniture	Fixtures	Equipment
Bed	Light switch	TV
Sofa	Air conditioning unit	Trouser press
Wardrobe	Air vents	Telephone
Desk and chairs	Bath tub	Safe
Arm chair	Vanity unit	Mini bar
Coffee table	Mirror	
Bedside table	**Case goods**	
	Carpet	
	Windows	
	Toilet	
	Curtains	

DEFINITION

Case goods – items with tops and sides for example wardrobes, luggage racks and drawers.

Using the inventory list, the executive housekeeper then identifies the *frequency* of cleaning of each item, as not all items require cleaning on a daily basis.

Step 2 – task list

A *task list* of what jobs needs to be completed when cleaning a room, is then created.

- Clean desk
- Wipe plants
- Vacuum carpet
- Polish TV
- Clean bath
- Clean a table
- Polish mirror
- Polish windows
- Dust telephone
- Change bed

- Empty bins
- Change coffee cups
- Polish taps
- Open curtains
- Disinfect toilet
- Check light bulbs
- Enter room
- Fresh towels

After creating a list of tasks they need to be put into the correct order to be completed.

Put these tasks into the most logical order from entering the room to leaving the room.

1, 2, 3, 4

The above list of tasks is *just an idea* to get you thinking about the process of organising cleaning. The list of tasks change:

- Depending on the standard of hotel
- The standard of hotel room (standard, junior suite, executive room)
- If it was a check-out or a stay-over room
- The amount of facilities available in the room
- The budget available for cleaning

The main concept is that the cleaning needs to be carried out in a *particular chronological order*. Failing to do this could increase the total time to clean.

Note: Whilst cleaning of the room is of utmost importance, additional care and attention needs to be given to the correct positioning of furniture to create a good overall impression.

In many high quality hotels the housekeeping department maintains records on the likes and dislikes of regular customers in relation to room layout. For example, Mr Akamura, a regular visitor to the hotel, prefers the desk to be located closer to the window. Therefore, prior to Mr Akamura's arrival, the desk will be moved to meet his specific needs.

BPP
LEARNING MEDIA

ACTIVITY 2   **20 minutes**

Room attendants' trolleys contribute to the organisation and efficiency of work.

List 15 items that would be found on a room attendant's trolley.

3.2 Recyclable and non-recyclable items

Housekeeping inventory items can be organised into recyclable and non-recyclable, examples of which are given below.

Recyclable	Non-recyclable
Towel	Shampoo
Bed sheet	Soap
Pillow case	Toilet paper

ACTIVITY 3   **20 minutes**

What are the main *recyclable* and *non-recyclable* inventory items that are the responsibility of the Housekeeping department?

Step 3 – how to perform each task

For each task previously detailed a *'Performance Standard'* needs to be created. Each standard should detail:

- Cleaning steps – The first step is to... 'put on gloves'

- A detailed description of each cleaning step – wipe the toilet seat, using a blue cloth in a circular motion removing all hairs and stains

- Exact measurements of any cleaning agents – add 2ml of disinfectant to the cloth

- Timings for each step – this step will take one minute

- Health and Safety information – before mixing read label

Figure 2.1 gives an example of a performance standard. The advantages of having a standard for each task is.

- It can be used as a *training* document for new employees
- Specific instructions guide the employee, *minimising errors*
- All employees follow the standard which results in *consistency*
- It can be used as a *checking tool* for supervisors
- Visible pictures benefit overseas employees
- It can in some situations be translated into the language of the workforce
- It accurately costs tasks which allow for better *financial control*
- Clear break-down provides for enhanced *quality control*

Step		Time
1	Put on gloves	
2	Put 1oz of detergent on blue cloth and wipe cistern, handle, sides and on top of lid removing all stains	1 minute
3	Lift lid and thoroughly wipe on top and below seat with wetted blue cloth and a dash of detergent.	1 minute
4	Using a toilet brush in a circular motion brush inside of toilet bowl with 1 ounce of bleach.	1 minute
5	Rinse cloth and wipe exterior of toilet bowl .	.30
6	Flush once. Deposit 1 cap of bleach in toilet bowl.	.15
7	Place disposable toilet cover on seat	.15
8	Place full toilet roll in holder, envelope ends	
	Total cleaning time	4 minutes

Resources Required	
1 set	Rubber gloves
1	Blue cloth/toilet brush
1 btl.	Bleach
1 btl.	Detergent

Figure 2.1: Example of a performance standard

3.3 Productivity standard – how long?

Kappa et al. (1997) explain that productivity standards ask "How long should it take for a housekeeping employee to perform an assigned task according to the department's performance standard?"

As given in Figure 2.1, the estimated time to clean a toilet should be around four minutes. Through *adding all the tasks* individually this should equate to the *total time* to clean a room.

Note: A check-out room would require longer cleaning than a stay-over room.

ACTIVITY 4   30 minutes

As a floor housekeeper explain how would you deal with the following situation.

Estimated room cleaning time at the Montblanc Hotel is 35 minutes. However:

- One room attendant has finished their room in 25 minutes
- One room attendant has finished their room in 45 minutes

ACTIVITY 5   50 minutes

Carry out your own research (via internet, book and personal contact) to create performance standards for the following housekeeping tasks.

- Making a guest room bed
- Vacuuming a hotel bedroom
- Carrying out an evening 'turn down' service

BPP LEARNING MEDIA

4 Public area cleaning

It is not only the bedrooms that require cleaning. Public area cleaning includes:

- Restaurants
- Bars
- Conference and Banqueting
- Health club
- Lobby
- Corridors
- Lifts
- Public toilets

Establishing and maintaining housekeeping procedures for public areas is just as important as it is for guest rooms, but much less standardised. The housekeeping needs of public areas vary considerably among properties because of architectural differences, lobby space allocations, activities, and guest traffic. These and other factors also affect scheduling routines, requiring many of the cleaning tasks to be performed at night or on a special project basis.   *Kappa et al. (1997)*

4.1 Food and Beverage cleaning

The cleaning of food and beverage areas is in most cases a partnership between housekeeping and food service personnel, with the managers of each section agreeing on their respective cleaning responsibilities.

For example, perhaps within a lounge bar the food and beverage personnel would be responsible for maintaining the lounge tables, cushions, sofas and bar area, whereby the housekeeping personnel would vacuum, polish brass fixtures, clean windows and maintain plants. The importance is not who does what as long as one department is given responsibility. Although, some responsibility may be given to food and beverage personnel the executive housekeeper is still responsible overall, and will carry out routine checks to ensure the areas are being cleaned appropriately.

Most food and beverage cleaning is carried out at off peak or night time, when there is least demand for service.

It is important for the executive housekeeper to monitor special events around the hotel, such as conferences and functions, as this creates more demand for cleaning. A sports event being televised in the bar is normally a popular attraction and would create more demand on the housekeeping function, such as higher supervision of public toilets throughout the evening.

4.2 Lobby and other Public Areas cleaning

Within these areas duties include vacuuming, polishing floors, organising cushions, wiping tables, polishing mirrors, cleaning plants, emptying bins and ashtrays and polishing brass fittings.

4.3 Front Entrance cleaning

This area is '*the first impression and the last impression*' for most visitors and so it is imperative that it is clean and presentable at all times. The appearance of the approach and entrance is also important and so wiping hand smudges from doors, sweeping leaves and removing debris are some of the tasks required to be carried out. Poor weather conditions require additional monitoring and cleaning throughout the day.

4.4 Pest control

An ongoing, proactive pest control program is imperative in order to maintain customer satisfaction and a healthy reputation.

"The biggest pest threats to hotel accommodation areas are bedbugs and other biting insects."

Rentokil UK (2009)

Visit the Rentokil website for further information:
http:www.rentokil.co.uk/commercial-pest-control/your-business/hotels/

4.5 Public Toilets cleaning

Customers can have a lovely meal in the restaurant but if the toilet they have to use is unclean it can have a negative impact on the whole visit. Refilling toilet rolls, paper hand towels and soap dispensers, emptying bins, cleaning of toilets, hand basins and mirrors and regular mopping are just some of the checks required throughout the day.

FOR DISCUSSION

As an executive housekeeper how would you ensure that public toilets are kept clean and well stocked at all times.

5 Staff scheduling

Ensuring that you staff correctly is essential for any manager. If too many employees are scheduled then this is waste and costing standards are jeopardised. The following factors are considerations that an executive housekeeper needs to consider when preparing a week's rota.

- Room occupancy
- Labour budget available
- Type of room to be cleaned
- Stay-over or check-out
- Customer profile
- Employee holidays
- Turndown service

- Check-in time/check-out time
- Special requests
- Skill level of employees
- Public areas and frequency of cleaning
- Supervision
- Special events taking place in hotel

A C T I V I T Y   6   **2 0   m i n u t e s**

Hotel Splendid is a budget hotel with 100 rooms and few public areas. It takes 30 minutes on average to clean a room.

How many room attendants would be required each day based on the occupancy in the table below?

	Mon	Tues	Weds	Thurs	Fri	Sat	Sun
% occupancy	42%	60%	65%	71%	90%	100%	22%
Staff required	?	?	?	?	?	?	?

A C T I V I T Y   7   **2 0   m i n u t e s**

You are a human resources training officer. Please design and prepare a general property information pack and a Housekeeping department induction pack for a room attendant starting work in a 200-room, 3-star hotel, in your city.

SUMMARY

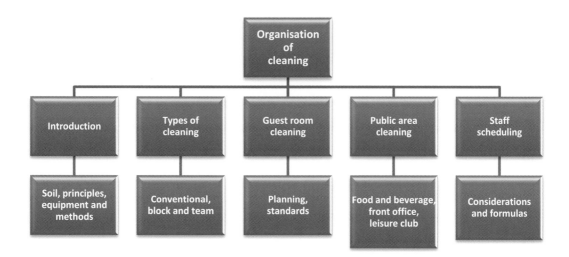

SELF-TEST QUESTIONS

1 What are the names of two types of soil?

2 Provide two ways that soil from outside could be prevented from entering the hotel.

3 What type of cleaning is it when the employee moves from room to room and completes the same task in every room?

4 Carpet shampooing is an example of what type of cleaning?

5 True or False – an in-room inventory is a description of how to clean a room.

6 True or False – a 'task list' is a list of the order of tasks when cleaning a room.

7 What are the benefits of a performance standard?

8 What is the purpose of a productivity standard?

9 Which department is normally responsible for cleaning food and beverage areas?

10 What factors contribute to the frequency of cleaning a lobby area?

SELF-TEST ANSWERS

1 Organic and inorganic

2 Mats, foot scrubs, bins

3 Block cleaning

4 Deep cleaning

5 False, an in-room inventory is a list of all items in a room that need to be cleaned

6 True

7 Consistency, quality control, used for training, guidance, cost control

8 To allocate a desired cleaning time per task to maintain efficiency

9 A combination of food and beverage and housekeeping personnel

10 Weather, traffic, hotel events

ANSWERS TO ACTIVITIES

1

■	Brushes	Sweeping leaves and dusty floors
■	Chamois leather	Cleaning hotel vehicles
■	Dusters	In room dusting of fixtures and furniture
■	Dustpan and brush	In the bar to deal with glass breakage
■	Mop and bucket	In kitchen to mop up spillages
■	Ladders	High dusting, window cleaning (normally carried out by external company)
■	Trolleys	Moving laundry or heavy waste bags
■	Squeegee	Window cleaning
■	Sprayers	Applying chemicals on surfaces
■	Vacuum cleaners	Vacuuming carpet in bedrooms and restaurants
■	Wet vacuums	Shampooing carpets
■	Wet extractors	Dealing with floods, weather or heavy leaks
■	Rotary machines	Polishing marble floors

2 May include:

- Cleaning caddy
- Towels
- Bed linen
- Stationery
- Dustbin
- Laundry bag
- Dustpan and brush
- Dustbin

- Vacuum cleaner
- Disinfectant
- Polish
- Cleaning cloths
- Air freshener
- Room Status report
- Sharps box

3

Recyclable	Non-recyclable
■ Towel	■ Shampoo
■ Face towel	■ Soap
■ Bath sheet	■ Toilet paper
■ Pillow case	■ Moisturisers
■ Duvet cover	■ Conditioners
■ Mattress cover	■ Sewing kits
■ Bed sheet	■ Shoe shine kits
■ Shower curtains	■ Chemicals
■ Curtains	
■ Bathrobes	
■ Slippers	

4 **One room attendant has finished their room in 25 minutes**

Check that all standards have been followed with no short cuts. If a cleaner has finished earlier it may be just that the customer has left little mess and therefore less to clean.

One room attendant has finished their room in 45 minutes

Check that the cleaner is working to the correct speed per cleaning task. Some room customers make a lot of mess and hence the room requires more time to clean.

5 The answer to this activity depends on your own research.

6 Monday

42% occupancy = 42 rooms

30 minutes cleaning per room

Therefore, cleaning minutes required = 42 × 30 = 1,260 minutes.

Total cleaning hours = 1,260 ÷ 60 = 21

Assume each cleaner works a 7.5 hour shift.

Therefore, 21 ÷ 7.5 = 2.8 full-time room attendants required to carry out the room cleaning.

Note that this does not take into consideration early check-outs or arrivals.

Similar calculations give the following requirements for the rest of the week:

	Mon	Tues	Weds	Thurs	Fri	Sat	Sun
% occupancy	42%	60%	65%	71%	90%	100%	22%
Staff required	42 x 30 minutes = 1,260 mins ÷ 60 = 21 hours of cleaning ÷ 7.5 shift = 2.8 staff	4	4.3	4.7	6	6.6	1.5

7 **Could include**

- Tour of hotel
- Who's who
- Background to company
- Contract information
- Employee handbook
- General brand standards
- Specific brand standards for position
- Making a bed
- Using chemicals
- Cleaning a room
- Using specific equipment
- Speaking with customers
- Team work
- Health and safety

CHAPTER 3

FURNITURE, FIXTURES AND FABRIC

Chapter objectives

By the end of this chapter you will be able to

- Describe some of the factors that you would need to consider when selecting flooring
- Identify the main considerations when selecting furnishings
- Identify the main fixtures and equipment you would find in hotel bedrooms
- Outline some general design considerations for hotel properties
- Design a hotel bedroom

Topic list
Introduction to design
Purchasing considerations of capital expenditure items
Housekeeping design considerations

Source: http://www.silkroadandbeyond.co.uk

1   Introduction to design

Hotels and their facilities are designed in many different ways. Hotels can either be unique in their design or similar throughout one chain. When designing hotels many different considerations need to be taken into account, for example:

- That customers receive the best aesthetic experience
- The appropriate design meets practical and safety requirements
- It meets the requirements of the target market
- It is cost effective
- Its maintenance requirements

Casado (2000). "Regardless of their type of service, lodging properties must maintain interior design consistency standards throughout the building. Whether a property has been classified as economy, mid-market, or luxury, its guest rooms and public area design, colour patterns, fabric and upholstery, and overall appearance must benefit the category they represent".

Raghubalan and Raghubalan (2007) explain that design can be divided into two main types, structural and decorative. Structural design is comprised of the size, form, colour, and texture of an object. Decorative design – any lines, colour, or materials that have been applied to structural design for the purpose of adding a richer quality to it constitute its decorative design.

1.1   Design

- Creates atmosphere
- Communicates image
- Underpins the hotel theme
- Is the first impression
- Presents the standard
- Communicates where in the life cycle the hotel is positioned

FOR DISCUSSION

Look at the following images of hotel bedrooms. Evaluate their design in relation to:

- First impression
- Visual impact
- Co-ordination of colour, texture and shape
- Who the room is targeting
- Any weaknesses

Sources

http://www.channel4.com

http://www.dezeen.com

http://www.millionface.com

http://www.tallmanhotel.com

http://www.boston.com

http://leegrantphotography.files.wordpress.com

Figure 3.1: Different types of hotel design

As shown above, hotels can adopt different themes of design; some hotels aim to be modern and stylish, whereby others' like to remain old and authentic such as old country inns. Hotels aimed at tourists design their facilities to fit in with the local culture to provide guests with a fuller experience of the destination. The chain of Hard Rock Hotels theme their rooms around rock music with various music memorabilia on show.

Source: http://www.gearfuse.com

BPP))) LEARNING MEDIA

ACTIVITY 1   20 minutes

Visit the web sites of the following themed hotels

- Hard Rock Hotel
  Website http://www.hardrockhotels.net

- Ice Hotel
  Website http://www.icehotel.com

- Disney Hotel
  Website http://disneyland.disney.go.com

Furthermore, hotels are, in most cases, designed to meet the needs of a particular target market, as given in the following table.

Target market	Design features
Business traveller	In-room (Wi-Fi, desk, satellite TV with news channels, trouser press, safe, iPod dock, warmer colours used to decorate walls and furnishings)
Female traveller	In-room (Extra wardrobe space, extra hangers, large vanity, full length mirror, softer colours used in design and furnishings, hairdryer, secure lock)
Families	In-room (sofa bed, cartoon channel, X Box, video channel, emphasis on safety, no sharp furniture edges)

Thought also needs to be given to visitors with differing disabilities and special needs and requirements.

ACTIVITY 2   30 minutes

What special in-room facilities would be needed for:

- Wheelchair customers
- Visually impaired customers
- Hearing impaired customers

2 Purchasing considerations of capital expenditure items

Capital expenditure items are objects of large expense (fixed assets) that are purchased. Examples include furniture, equipment and decoration. When purchasing these items many factors need to be considered as illustrated below and examined in more detail in the table following.

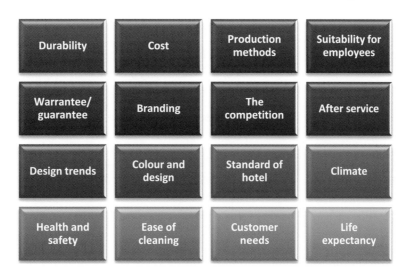

Considerations	Examples
Durability/life expectancy	On selecting items consideration needs to be given to the amount of usage the item will have. Purchasing cheap, flimsy products will not withstand commercial use and therefore it is better to purchase durable, strong, simple products.
Cost	When purchasing you need to consider funds available and the potential return on investment. Ensure three quotations are obtained from suppliers to get the best deal. It is better to invest money in assets that will have a longer life.
Production method	Many consumers are now interested in how products are produced and made, such as purchasing fair trade, organic cotton, using local tradespeople as opposed to flying products in from overseas.
Suitability for employees	It is important to consider the practicality of furniture and equipment for employees. If furniture is too heavy staff will have problems moving it.
Warrantee/guarantee/ after-service	Is there after-service available if the purchase breaks? Due to the nature of hotels the volume of customers passing through can easily damage in-room assets, which require replacements etc. Similarly, equipment such as vacuum cleaners being used constantly can easily break down.
Branding	Some hotels, when decorating and purchasing fabrics and linen, consider the overall branding, for example the colour of the logo of Premier Travel Inn, the UK budget hotel chain, is purple. On entering a room in this chain the carpets, bed sheets and decor is in theme with the colours of the logo.
Competition	The design features the hotel adopts can be used as a differentiator against competitors. Many customers will select one hotel over another if the design is different
Trends	Hotels who want to remain competitive need to keep up-to-date with external design trends to ensure customers are retained.
Colour and design	Colours, textures, consistency all need to be considered when purchasing capital items for rooms and public areas. If colours are in stark contrast or very different it does not look attractive to the eye.
Hotel standard	The amount the hotel spends on capital assets should be representative of the standard and quality of the hotel.
Climate	Climate is a big consideration. In hotter climates fresh, light colours, cool tiles, air conditioning are required. In cooler climates, warm colours, heating and carpets.
Health and Safety	Health and Safety needs to be paramount when purchasing items. Portable appliance testing and flame spread index are examples to be considered.
Customer needs	As discussed previously, different target customers have different requirements which need to be incorporated into the in-room and public area design.

3 Housekeeping design considerations

Housekeeping design considerations mainly concentrate on in-room design and public areas. We will now consider in more depth the following areas of design:

3.1 Flooring

Walking around the hotel various floorings can be seen. *Raghubalan and Raghubalan (2007)* explain that 'floors are an important aspect of hotel interiors as they are both functional and decorative. The guest's first impression of an hotel is largely determined by the appearance of the flooring in the lobby, the guest corridors, restaurants and guest rooms'.

FOR DISCUSSION

Which types of flooring would be most suitable for the following areas within an hotel, and why?

- A bathroom
- A main kitchen
- A hotel lobby
- An office
- A gymnasium
- A conference room
- Dishwashing area
- Car park
- A bar
- A nightclub

What needs to be considered?

- **Cost**: cheap is usually uneconomical. Account for initial purchase cost, cost of laying, maintenance costs and life expectancy.

- **Durability and quality**: **traffic flows** – different types of floor are appropriate in different circumstances. Consideration needs to be given to preventing entry of dirt not just to maintain cleanliness, but to prevent damage to flooring (grit, grease, water).

- **Appearance**: interior design needs to be considered as well as the purpose of the area. Colour, texture and pattern requires thought in relation to **FFE**. Flooring is usually chosen first because of size, cost and the fact it will be changed less frequently than décor and furniture.

DEFINITION

FFE – Furniture, Fixtures and Equipment.

- **Safety**: should have non-slip qualities when wet, or dry to avoid slips and falls. Correct cleaning and maintenance helps improve safety.

- **Comfort**: not just underfoot; noise needs to be taken into account. Should be warm, soft, quiet and provide good heat and sound insulation.

Different types of flooring materials

Porous	Semi-porous	Non-porous
Wood	Thermoplastic	Terrazzo
Cork	Vinyl	Quarry tiles
Concrete	Linoleum	Ceramic tiles
Chipboard	Rubber	Stone/slate
Asphalt		Marble
Carpets		

ACTIVITY 3   40 minutes

Complete the table about different types of floor covering below.

	Advantages	Disadvantages
Carpets		
Marble		
Ceramic tiles		
Cement		
Linoleum		
Laminate		

"Floors are subjected to more wear than any other surface in hotels."

Raghubalan and Raghubalan (2007)

Carpets

Casado (2000) 'Beautiful carpeting can enhance the appearance of lodging properties and make a lasting impression on guests. On the other hand, discoloured, worn, or dirty carpets are usually sources of guest complaints'.

Advantages	Disadvantages
Luxurious	Requires regular cleaning
Durable	Absorbs dirt, stains and odours
Comfortable	Shading
Contributes to atmosphere	Pilling
Available in various designs, patterns and colours	Pile reversal
Insulation and noise absorbent	Shedding
Comfortable on feet for employees	Fading
Cushions breakages	Matting

Carpets have three components: an underlay, a backing, and a face as illustrated below.

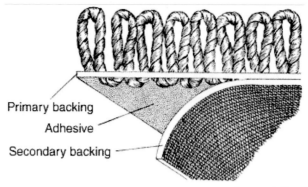

Primary backing
Adhesive
Secondary backing

Source: http://extension.missouri.edu

Figure 3.2: Carpet construction

Carpets can be constructed in different ways, all of which provide different levels of comfort.

SAXONY

- Smooth, soft cut pile surface
- Versatile in performance & in appearance
- Works well with traditional rooms

SHAG

- Surface helps hide footprints
- Great texture, fun, casual appearance
- Ideal for active families, used in any room

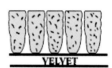

VELVET

- Fine, tip sheared surface
- Elegant style, very formal and traditional
- Classic Broadloom Construction

FRIEZE

- Textured surface, with knubby appearance
- Extremely durable, and long wearing
- Good for active rooms

RANDOM-SHEARED

- Distinctive carved appearance
- Cut and loops give a variety of surface levels
- Fits a variety of room settings

MUTLI-LEVEL LOOP

- Several different levels of loops
- Creates a unique looking pattern effect
- Casual or tailored appearance

LEVEL LOOP

- Loops are all the same height
- Casual appearance, but extremely durable
- Good for family, media, and home fitness rooms

Source: http://rminteriorsanddesign.com

Figure 3.3: Different carpet styles

ACTIVITY 4   30 minutes

Visit a local carpet store and research the following types of carpet production:

1	Woven	5	Saxony
2	Tufted	6	Wilton
3	Axminster	7	Persian rug
4	Oriental	8	Chinese rug

FOR DISCUSSION

What are some of the main uses for rugs within a hotel?

FOR DISCUSSION

Are carpets suitable for busy restaurants?

Tips for maintaining carpets

- Use mats to minimise dirt entry (clean mats regularly)
- Use effective vacuum cleaners
- Remove furniture regularly to prevent build-up of dirt
- Use carpet glides to prevent pile distortion
- Use blinds and curtains to minimise long-term sun damage
- Attend promptly to spillages and stains with spotting and treatment
- Periodic deep cleaning and shampooing
- Use mats on top of carpets in areas of heavy usage

3.2 Wall coverings

Source: http://designholeonline.com

Kappa et al. (1997) explain 'Ceiling, wall, and window coverings are chosen more for their acoustical properties, safety, and appearance than insulation against the cold. There is a wide variety of ceiling surfaces and wall coverings on the market today. Paint is by the most common. However, vinyl manufacturers have introduced a wide variety of practical and attractive products in recent years, making vinyl a popular alternative to paint in properties of all types'.

	Advantages	Disadvantages
Paint	Inexpensive, easy to clean, wide variety of colours available, durable, easy to apply	Easily chipped, marked, in-elegant
Vinyl	Wide variety of patterns, colours and designs, adds character, fashionable	Labour intensive to apply, not suitable for humid climates, damage cannot be rectified easily
Fabric	Elegant, warm, comfortable	Easily damaged, absorbs aromas, hard to clean, hard to erect

Type of wall covering	Method of cleaning
Wall carpet, felt, flock, grass, cloth, hessian and jute, linen, silk	Brush down with a soft, long-handled wall brush or use a vacuum cleaner with a brush attachment. To remove stains, dust lightly with white talc on cotton wool; leave for a few hours; then brush off. Do not use dry cleaning reagents or upholstery cleaners, as they may cause discoloration and shrinkage.
Cork	Brush or vacuum. Then sponge away any marks gently with lukewarm water and mild detergent. Do not over-wet.
Paint – emulsion	Wipe down with a sponge wrung out in warm water. Do not rub flock.
Paint – glossy, silk finish, vinyl	Wash wall from bottom upwards using a sponge wrung out in mild detergent solution; wipe residue with cold water, working from top down. If necessary, scrub gloss paint with a soft brush.
Tiles – aluminium and ceramic	Wipe down with a sponge wrung out in mild detergent solution; rinse well. Dry with chamois leather.
Tiles – mirror	Wipe down with a piece of chamois leather wrung out in vinegar water.
Wallpaper	Brush or lightly vacuum; then gently sponge away marks with a mild detergent solution. For grease stains, dab on white talc lightly with cotton wool and brush off after a few hours.
Wood panelling	Brush or vacuum and rub clean with soft dusters. Periodically apply teak oil or cream. Do not use wax polish.

Source: Raghubalan and Raghubalan (2007)

3.3 Furniture

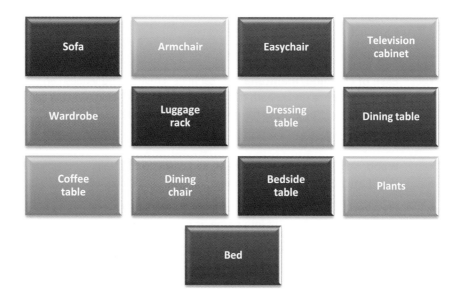

Types of furniture

- **Free standing**: can be moved or rearranged relatively easily. Accumulates dust/dirt, behind, above and beneath it.

- **Built-in**: eg wardrobes, kitchen furniture. This can be expensive. There should be no gaps underneath so cleaning is minimised.

- **Fitted**: includes items like shelves and headboards. Makes use of alcoves and recesses and so ensures good use of space. Not to be confused with built-in.

- **Cantilevered**: supported on only one end, can be quite effective from a design perspective.

- **Upholstered**: sofas, armchairs. Suitability of fabric needs to be considered, as does ease of cleaning and maintenance.

- **Antique**: usually very expensive, can be impractical, also risky as difficult to replace and repairs often need to be carried out by a specialist.

What factors need to be considered when selecting furniture?

- **Frequency of use**: needs to be durable and versatile.

- **Design and comfort**: should be pleasing to the eye and blend in with the area. Comfort is very important particularly in beds and seating.

- **Repair and replacement**: there is a difference between commercial and domestic furniture.

- **Ease of cleaning/maintenance**: carvings, crevices and ledges can be dust traps. There should be enough space underneath furniture to facilitate cleaning. Castors can help with moving of heavier items. Many chairs have removable, washable covers.

Wooden furniture

- **Wood**: solid wood can be expensive and costly to maintain. It is absorbent and stains easily. Most furniture is made from plywood, or laminated wood with a wood or plastic veneer.

- **Plywood**: is built-up from odd numbers of layers that run at right angles to each other. It is strong, can easily be bent into shape, is lighter than wood and can be made waterproof.

- **Laminated wood**: is also built-up from layers, but unlike plywood these run in the same direction. It is not as strong as plywood, and one piece can very easily be bent into curved shapes by steaming.

- **Chipboard**: made from wood chippings moulded and pressed together with steam and glue. Usually finished with a wood, or plastic veneer.

- **Veneers**: usually cut from the barks of trees. Once stuck down it gives the appearance of solid wood.

- **Plastics**: usually used in dining, or workroom areas. Plastic is lightweight, easy to clean and maintain It is durable and light to move, or stack.

Beds

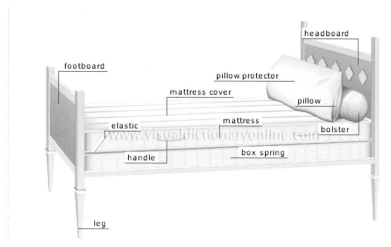

Source: http://visual.merriam-webster.com

"Beds are the central attraction in guest rooms and often a big selling point for travellers when choosing a lodging property".

Casado (2000)

Roll-away bed

Box frame

Metal frame beds

Cot

Four-poster bed

Sofa bed

Figure 3.4: Bed types

Sources:

http://www.absolutecomfortonsale.com
http://www.lakewoodconferences.com
http://www.kdbeds.com
http://www.bedsandbunks.co.uk
http://www.ukhomeideas.co.uk
http://www.alecs3piecesuites.co.uk

Mattress

Casado (2000) explains "surveys of favourite amenities conducted regularly by hospitality magazines consistently show that guests put comfortable mattresses at the top of the list". Differing types are given below.

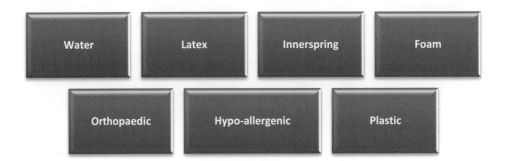

ACTIVITY 5   15 minutes

What are the different ways that mattresses can be maintained by the Housekeeping department?

UK bed and mattress sizes

Name	Width	Length (feet)
Bunk	3′	6′3″
Single	3′	6′3″
Double bed	4′6″	6′3″
King bed	5′	6′6″
Super King bed	6′	6′6″

3.4   Fixtures and fittings

Fixtures and fittings are items, as illustrated below, that are attached to the structure or pieces of furniture. Some of these items serve a purpose whereas others are simply for decoration and to create atmosphere. However, they require regular, ongoing cleaning.

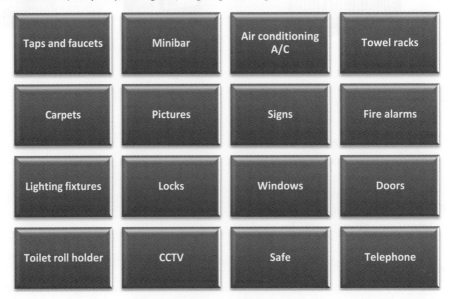

ACTIVITY 6   40 minutes

What are the names for the different types of furniture pictured below. Furthermore identify if they are case goods, cantilevered, upholstered etc.

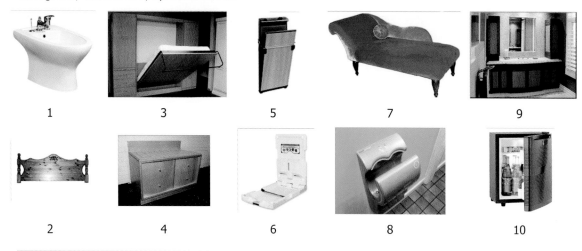

1	3	5	7	9
2	4	6	8	10

Sources:
http://www.global-b2b-network.com
http://www.cnmonline.co.ukl
http://www.petstreetmall.com
http://www.custommade.com
http://www.focusfurnishing.co.uk
http://www.cityfurnitureclearance.co.uk
http://www.ozifresh.com.
http://www.marramgrass.org.uk
http://img.archiexpo.com

Care considerations

Kappa et al. (1997) explains 'in general, major cleaning procedures include shampooing upholstered furnishings – usually about every six months or as needed – and cleaning washable furnishings with water and/or an appropriate cleaning solution. Most *major cleaning* can be performed with very simple tools – buckets, rags, and a cleaning agent. Upholstery shampoos, however, usually require special shampooers. *Minor cleaning* is performed more frequently than major cleaning. Minor cleaning includes such tasks as dusting and vacuuming lampshades and seat cushions and polishing metal fixtures. Paper dust cloths treated with furniture polish are generally used in dusting'.

ACTIVITY 7   30 minutes

What are the following housekeeping items?

Key word	Meaning – usage
Case goods	
Furniture glides	
Helical hooks	
Murphy bed	
Swag	
Vanity unit	
WHB	
Zed bed	
Castors	

3.5 Equipment

Equipment requirements vary depending on the hotel's:

- standard,
- type of room (standard, twin, executive, suite),
- size of room,
- target customer,
- budget available,
- theme,

but examples of typical in-room equipment are shown in the chart, below.

Casado (2000) explains 'long gone are the days when hoteliers could sell rooms equipped with a minimum of basic features. Today's business traveller is putting a new spin on the concept of guest room equipment. Lodging chains that cater to corporate clientele offer in-room or satellite office support services including computers and fax and copy machines. Guest rooms are often equipped with multi-line telephones complete with voice mail and PC compatibility'.

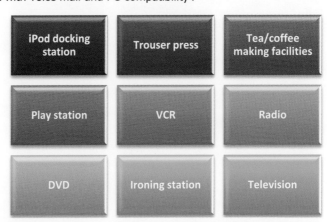

BPP
LEARNING MEDIA

FOR DISCUSSION

How would the in-room equipment vary in the different type of hotels listed below?

- Budget hotel
- Apartment hotel
- 4* hotel
- Luxury hotel

ACTIVITY 8   60 minutes

Scenario

You are the recently appointed Executive Housekeeper of the King George Hotel. The hotel is a new property and is due to open in May next year. The target markets for the hotel will be business travellers during the week and leisure travellers, (including families), at weekends. The hotel will be operating in the mid-price range and will have 250 standard bedrooms. The hotel will also have a bar, restaurant and coffee shop. There is also a leisure club, spa, beauty treatment rooms and children's outside play area. The hotel will purchase its own linen stock and use contract laundry services.

Your key responsibilities in the *pre-opening* phase are:

(a)   making recommendations to the designers regarding bedroom décor, furnishings and facilities; and

(b)   the development of procedures to ensure an efficient, high quality housekeeping service.

Floor plan

Create a floor plan of a standard bedroom detailing dimensions and lay out.

DESIGN

Make recommendations regarding the floor plan, facilities, flooring, lighting, furnishings (bedroom and bathroom), linen and décor in order to fully equip the bedroom. To support your recommendations you should provide a scale drawing of your floor plan, as well as samples and sketches of materials and illustrations. You should also calculate the cost of furnishing, decorating and equipping the room to your design. You must fully justify your choices in terms of:

- visual impact
- ambience
- appropriateness for market
- durability
- cost
- access and mobility
- airflow
- fire regulations
- DDA
- cleaning and maintenance

SUMMARY

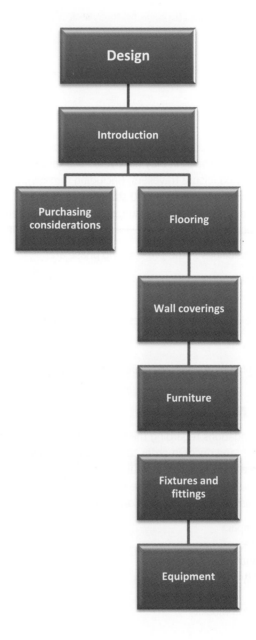

SELF-TEST QUESTIONS

1   True or False – design requirements are the same for all customers.

2   What is meant by capital expenditure?

3   Name the three components of a carpet.

4   Name any three advantages of carpets.

5   How would you clean a painted wall surface (emulsion paint)?

6   Where would you find a bidet?

7   What type of bed might be requested for a family of three staying in a room?

8   Name any three examples of fittings that you would find in a hotel bedroom.

9   Case furniture is in most cases made from what type of material?

10   What examples of in-room equipment would be found in a standard hotel room?

SELF-TEST ANSWERS

1 False – different customers have different needs

2 Capital expenditure is planned purchases of major assets

3 Underlay, backing and face

4 Could include – luxurious, durable, comfortable, contributes to atmosphere, available in various designs, patterns and colours, insulation, noise absorbent, comfortable on feet for employees, cushions breakages

5 Wipe down with a sponge wrung out in warm water

6 In a bathroom

7 A roll away/cot

8 Any from those given in section 3.4

9 Wood

10 TV, tea and coffee-making facilities, ironing board, radio, IPOD station

ANSWERS TO ACTIVITIES

1 There is no formal answer to this activity.

2 **Wheelchair customers**
- Wide frames on all door into and within the room
- Open Shower
- Bath with opening side door
- Low peep hole
- Low, eye level handles and fixtures within room

Visually impaired customers
- Room number in Braille
- All in room literature in Braille
- Good lighting
- Large fonts on literature
- Large numerals on in room telephone
- No obtrusive furniture

Hearing impaired customers
- Vibrating pillow for wake-up call
- Flashing light for visitors (instead of bell)

3

	Advantages	Disadvantages
Carpets	■ Luxurious feel ■ Comfortable on foot ■ Good insulator ■ Available in different colours and patterns ■ Noise reduction	■ Requires daily cleaning ■ Collects dirty ■ Requires shampooing from time to time ■ Can be expensive ■ Not suitable for all climates ■ When one section is damaged, the whole area needs replacing
Marble	■ Elegant first impression ■ Requires little cleaning ■ Durable, long lasting ■ Strong	■ Expensive ■ Slippery when wet
Ceramic Tiles	■ Available in different colours and patterns ■ Easy to clean	■ Difficult to replace when cracking
Cement	■ Strong ■ Durable ■ Non slip	■ Can crack which can cause accidents
Linoleum	■ Economical ■ Available in different colours and patterns ■ Easy to clean	■ When one section is damaged, the whole area needs replacing ■ Can be a poor reflection on establishment due to low cost
Laminate	■ Modern ■ Easy to clean ■ Relatively inexpensive	■ Slippery when wet ■ Cold ■ Can be noisy

4 There is no formal answer to this activity.

5
■ Turning mattress every 3 months
■ Airing mattresses
■ Mattress covers
■ Treating Stains promptly

6 Bidet, head board, murphy bed, luggage rack, trouser press, baby change, chaise longue, hot air blower, vanity unit, mini-bar.

7

Key word	Meaning – usage
Case goods	Furniture with a top and a side such as wardrobe, desk, luggage rack and drawers
Furniture glides	These are the wheels that are attached the furniture to assist in the careful transport of the furniture
Helical hooks	Are S shaped hooks that would be found on a flat spring mattress
Murphy bed	Beds that are built into walls to create additional space
Swag	Are the box like covers that would be situated at the head of curtains to cover the rails and add design
Vanity unit	The unit commonly found in the bathroom consisting of a shelf to store personal items and a large mirror
WHB	Wash Hand Basin
Zed bed	Portable folding bed that can be moved from room to room
Castors	Plastic objects that you place under sofa legs to protect the floor

8 **Making recommendations to the designers regarding bedroom décor, furnishings and facilities.**

Discuss:
- Target Market
- Hotel standard
- Budget
- Visual impact
- Ambience
- Appropriateness for market
- Durability
- Cost
- Access and mobility
- Airflow
- Fire regulations
- DDA

The development of procedures to ensure an efficient, high quality housekeeping service.

- Effective Leadership
- Standards of Performance
- Effective Human Resources (Recruitment, Training and Incentives)
- Quality Sourcing
- Effective Service Recovery and Complaint Handling
- Quality Schemes
- Quality Feedback and Monitoring Systems
- Mystery Visits

Floor plan

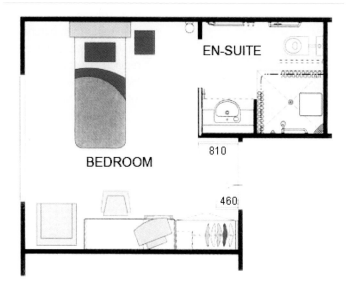

Source: http://www.maygroveorewa.co.nz

Recommendations regarding design.

▪	**Visual impact**	Ensure colours of furniture, fixtures and equipment coordinate and are pleasing to the eye
▪	**Ambience**	Consider the expectations of target market. Business customers require a soothing environment, quiet and convenient facilities.
▪	**Appropriateness for market**	Consider trends in business hotels design, furniture and equipment needs for the target market
▪	**Durability**	As hotel will target families on the weekends ensure design is safe and durable
▪	**Cost**	The cost of the design is reflected in the target market which is then incorporated into the pricing structures of the room. Therefore if you are attracting budget travellers expensive, stylishly designed furniture would not be purchased as it may need replacing frequently and it would take longer to recover investment in design asset.
▪	**Access and mobility**	Ensure that there is enough space to move around without feeling too cramped. What type of space would be required for business customers, meeting area, desk etc.
▪	**Airflow**	Consider conditioning, drafts and air flow when designing to create a comfortable atmosphere.
▪	**Fire regulations**	By law fire would need to be considered. When designing room layout consider best location for fire equipment that will not impact design features or accessing a negative way
▪	**DDA**	Most hotels have a number of rooms equipped to meet the needs of customers who may have a disability. For example customers in a wheelchair would require wider door frames and lower facilities

- **Cleaning & Maintenance**

How frequently do our customers require cleaning to meet their standard, to meet this standard what facilities are required. When purchasing furniture, fixtures and equipment ensure that they will be easy to maintain, replace and that they are durable. Children can damage assets when active, so safety and reducing the opportunity for breakage should be considered when purchasing items.

CHAPTER 4

HEALTH, SAFETY AND SECURITY

Chapter objectives

By the end of this chapter you will be able to

- Identify the main legislation relating to Health and Safety in the workplace
- Explain some of the main points relating to each of these laws
- Highlight some of the Health and Safety risks in the workplace and suggests steps which could be taken to minimise these
- Explain the importance of security to customers
- Identify some security risks that might be found in an hotel
- Carry out a risk assessment
- Detail the main health and safety considerations in operating leisure facilities

Source: http://www.westsomersetonline.gov.uk

Kappa et al. (1997) explain 'the two hotel departments most prone to accidents and injuries are maintenance and housekeeping'.

A C T I V I T Y   1   **3 0   m i n u t e s**

Consider some of the health, safety and security risks to the following groups of people

- Hotel customers
- Housekeeping employees

1 The importance of health, safety and security

Positive	Negative
Good image	Poor image (bad publicity)
Safe environment	Unsafe environment
Accident free	Frequent accidents
Employee satisfaction and retention	Employee dissatisfaction and turnover
Increased profits and productivity	Lost profit and low productivity
No law suits and insurance claims	Law suits and claims
Attract and retain customers	Lose customers

Figure 4.1: Maslow's Hierarchy of Needs

As shown in *Abraham Maslow's* famous model, illustrated above, personal safety and security is of great importance to individuals.

Kappa et al. (1997) explain 'In a hospitality operations, safety refers to the actual conditions in a work environment. Security refers to the prevention of theft, fire and other emergencies'.

It is the hotel's responsibility to provide a safe and secure environment for:

- Its customers and their belongings
- Its employees and their belongings
- The owner's assets

1.1 Who is responsible?

Although safety and security is everyone's responsibility, the General Manger is ultimately accountable. However, to assist in achieving a safe and secure environment, the following could be considered.

- Including the responsibility of safety into the job description of the Facilities/Maintenance Manager.
- Creating a Health and Safety Committee with representation from each department.
- Appointing a Chief of Security.
- Outsourcing security guards from a specialist agency.

1.2 Communication

It is key that the individuals responsible for health, safety and security ensure that **all** employees have the correct knowledge pertaining to their area.
This can be achieved by:

- Ongoing training
- Creating standards to be adhered to
- Key areas of importance integrated into induction
- Management by walking around
- Structured courses to educate employees

2 Safety and security risks for customers

Safety risks	Example	Prevention
Fire	Internal fires, fires caused by customers, cigarettes, heaters, electrical equipment	▪ Internal fire detection system ▪ Sprinklers ▪ Fire evacuation notices ▪ Fire marshals ▪ Fire extinguishers ▪ Training
Infestation	▪ Bed bugs ▪ Mosquitoes ▪ Rodents	▪ Good housekeeping ▪ Ongoing pest control programme
Trips/falls	▪ In-room falls ▪ Weather conditions ▪ Slippery lobby ▪ Defective flooring ▪ Obtrusive furniture	▪ Prompt repair ▪ Preventative maintenance ▪ Close off unsafe areas ▪ Wet floor signs ▪ Matting ▪ Non-slip matting in bathtubs ▪ Don't leave room service trays in corridors ▪ Rails ▪ Gritting
Pollution	Smoke inhalation from bars and nightclubs	▪ Good extraction ▪ Effective HVAC system
Faulty equipment/ electrical/ maintenance	▪ Boiling water ▪ Shorts in equipment	▪ Maintenance repair ▪ Preventative maintenance programme ▪ Purchase safe, tested equipment ▪ Portable appliance testing ▪ Risk assessment
Contamination	Potential for food contamination or from employees and individuals with viruses or disease	▪ HACCP ▪ Food safety testing ▪ Monitoring
Burns and scalds	▪ Burns from hot equipment ▪ Boiling water supply ▪ Exposed pipes	▪ Good maintenance ▪ Warning signage ▪ Communication from employees ▪ First aid procedures

Security risks		
Harassment/ attacks	Harassment from other customers	▪ Visible in-house security guards
Terrorist attacks	Suspicious packages	▪ Visible in-house security ▪ Crisis plan ▪ Awareness by employees
Fraudulent practices	▪ Employees attempting to defraud customers ▪ Identity theft	▪ Employ good staff – references/police checks ▪ Effective supervision ▪ CCTV ▪ Standards ▪ Data protection
Burglary/theft	▪ Potential theft from intruders, other customers or employees ▪ Misuse of guest room keys ▪ Giving out guest names/ or room numbers ▪ Theft of guest property ▪ Car theft	▪ Effective in-house security ▪ Awareness by employees ▪ Educating customers ▪ Use of in-room safes ▪ Safety deposit box ▪ Reference checks ▪ Guest key procedures ▪ CCTV ▪ Identity badges for agency staff ▪ Proper key control ▪ Signing in and out for all visitors ▪ Reporting of all damaged locks

DEFINITION

Data Protection – The protection of customers' personal information. A good example of how hotels need to adhere to this act is provided by McDonald Hotels and Resorts, reproduced below.

McDonald Hotels and Resorts Privacy Policy

Under the Data Protection Act 1998, we have a legal duty to protect any personal information we collect from you.

- We will only use personal information you supply to us for the purpose of contacting you.

- We will only hold your information for as long as necessary to fulfil that purpose.

- We will not pass your information to any other parties.

- All employees who have access to your personal data or are associated with the handling of that data are obliged to respect your confidentiality.

DEFINITION

Portable Appliance Testing – It is the responsibility of the employer to take necessary steps to ensure all equipment is safe. For more information on portable appliance testing see:

http://www.pat-testing.info

DEFINITION

Crisis Plan – This is a documented set of procedures and instructions on how managers should deal with emergency situations, for example terrorist attacks, force majeure, death should they in the unfortunate event, arise.

3 Health and Safety risks for Housekeeping employees

The Health and Safety Executive states in their workplace health and safety statistics that:

- There has been an increase in the rate of reported major and over-3-day injuries in the hotels and restaurant industry from 1999/2000 to 2007/08.

- Relative to other industries, a higher proportion of reported injuries in hotels and restaurants were caused by contact with harmful substances, electricity and exposure to fire.

The following chart shows typical health and safety risks for housekeeping employees.

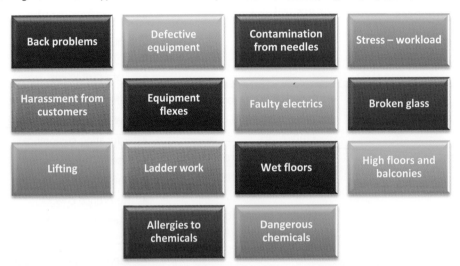

Risks	Examples	Prevention
Back problems	<ul><li>Turning mattresses</li><li>Pushing trolleys</li><li>Bending</li><li>Stretching</li></ul>	<ul><li>Training in lifting techniques</li><li>Ask for assistance</li></ul>
Dealing with hazardous chemicals	In most cases all Housekeeping employees will have to deal with chemicals at some point in time. The correct use of these chemicals is paramount and failing to do this can lead to serious injury.	<ul><li>COSHH training</li><li>Protective clothing</li><li>MSDS sheets</li></ul>
Defective equipment	Shorts in equipment	<ul><li>Maintenance repair</li><li>Preventative maintenance programme</li><li>Purchase safe, tested equipment</li><li>Portable appliance testing</li><li>Risk assessment</li></ul>
Contamination from infected needles/blood	Use of controlled substances in rooms by customers, or non-disposal of used needles. Hepatitis B virus or HIV found in infected blood are spread when blood or certain body fluids get into the body. This can occur through sharing needles and sexual contact.	Special training and standards in the correct, safe disposal of needles and blood stains in 'sharps boxes'

Work stress	All employees can be subject to additional work load and pressures which can lead to stress	▪ Good scheduling ▪ Regular breaks ▪ Job chats ▪ Fair distribution and allocation of work ▪ Observation **(MBWA)**
Equipment flexes	Room attendants frequently use equipment with long flexes and can be at risk of trips and falls	▪ Training ▪ Operating procedures
Wet/slippery floors	When floors are wet after mopping or wet weather	▪ Non-slip work shoes ▪ Wet floor signs ▪ Grit
High floor/ladder work	Some high dusting may require the use of ladders	▪ Training ▪ Ensure ladder is safe ▪ Colleague to hold ladder ▪ Only attempt if qualified ▪ Work at height regulation 2005 ▪ Never use chair instead of ladder
Broken glass/china	Room attendants and Public Area cleaners can come into contact with broken glass	Training/awareness/standards for correct disposal/broken glass containers
Office work	It is not only subordinates who face risks. Managers/operators who work at computers also can suffer from back pain, Repetitive and Strain Injury (RSI)	Provide an ergonomic workplace environment
Harassment from customers	On occasions employees can be at risk from customers over disputes	▪ Good security ▪ Awareness ▪ Training ▪ Complaint-handling procedures

DEFINITION

MBWA – Management by Walking Around. A management approach which focuses on frequently walking around the hotel to observe activities and ensure standards are being maintained.

3.1 Security of customers and their assets

To follow are some measures that can be taken to enhance security of customers and their assets when staying in hotels.

▪ Only issue room keys to registered guests

▪ Never disclose customers' room numbers to other guests

▪ Provide in-room safe boxes or safety deposit boxes in the main reception, and encourage customers to use them

▪ Provide peep holes on bedroom doors

▪ Provide double locks on bedroom doors

- When cleaning the room, always block door with trolley to prevent any unauthorised people for entering.

- If on cleaning a room the customer returns, ask for room card identification

- When allocating guest rooms, reservations should consider specific security needs of particular types of customers. Female travellers rate security and safety of great importance while travelling and staying in hotels. With this in mind, some hotels now provide a 'Female Floor' for female travellers to make them feel more safe.

- Have clear standards for chambermaids on lost property.

4 Prevention and legislation

The following chart provides some strategies to create a healthy, safe and secure hotel environment.

4.1 The Health and Safety at Work Act (HASAWA) 1974

The Act details:

- Provide and maintain plant and systems of work that are safe and without risk to health

- Ensure that the use, handling, storage and transport of articles or substances is safe and without risk

- Provide information, training and supervision to ensure that employees can carry out their jobs safely

- Ensure safe access and egress from the workplace. Ensure that the workplace is safe, particularly in respect of housekeeping, cleanliness, disposal of rubbish and stacking of goods

- Employers need to keep an up-to-date, written safety policy which is brought to the attention of employees

- Employers have a duty to consult with recognised safety representatives

- Employers must agree to establish a safety committee if requested by two, or more safety representatives   (HSE)

Web site: Also see the US Occupational Safety and Health Administration (OSHA) for more useful information on health and safety in the workplace.

http://www.osha.gov/

4.2 Manual Handling Regulations 1992

The Manual Handling Regulations 1992 are legislation that ensures that risks are reduced when moving or lifting heavy loads or equipment. This can include providing equipment to move and lift heavy goods and supplying the necessary training to employees on how to lift correctly, as illustrated below.

Figure 4.2: Lifting techniques

- Do not attempt to lift anything too heavy
- Bend your knees
- Keep back straight
- Firm grip
- Use legs to take the weight

Website: For more information on manual handling visit http://www.hse.gov.uk/pubns/manlinde.htm

4.3 Ergonomics – a safe office environment

Housekeeping **office personnel** also face health risks, which can lead to dissatisfaction and sickness. To reduce the opportunity of this, employers can provide their employees with an **ergonomic work environment** which makes work more safe and comfortable for employees.

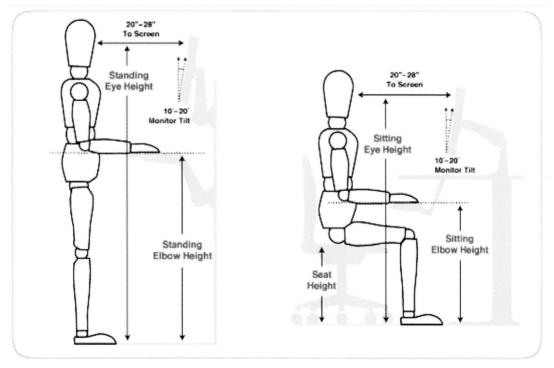

Source: http://www.infologix.com/

Figure 4.3: Example of ergonomic work environment

Example	Solution
Back pain from sitting at computers incorrectly and for long periods of time	Strong, adjustable, comfortable chairs. Adjustable desks/regular breaks
Eye strain form computer visual display units (VDU) screens	Screen covers for VDU to reduce glare and sore eyes/regular breaks
	Health and Safety (Display Screen Equipment) Regulations 1992
Repetitive Strain Injury (RSI)	Ergonomic mouse and wrist rests/regular breaks

Website: For more information and guidance for employers preventing back pain and employees dealing with back pain see http://www.hse.gov.uk/msd/backpain/employers.htm

4.4 Control of Substances Hazardous to Health (COSHH) 2002

Housekeeping and laundry employees are required to use chemicals in carrying out their day-to-day work tasks. According to The Health and Safety Executive 'Using chemicals or other hazardous substances at work can put people's health at risk, causing diseases including asthma, dermatitis or cancer. COSHH regulations require employers to control substances that can harm workers health'. COSHH legislation is there to protect the employee from dangerous chemicals within the workplace. and includes procedures for the correct:

- Storage and ventilation
- Mixing
- Application
- Pouring and measurement
- Labelling
- Training

http://safety-signs-catalogue.com

4.5 Material Safety Data Sheet (MSDS)

MSDS sheets are information pages that accompany each chemical, so the user is aware of the following.

- The chemical identity and what it contains
- What it is used for
- What the correct concentrations for different applications are
- Its toxic properties or special safety instructions for use
- Safety procedures if one gets chemical in contact with skin, eyes, or ingests it
- An emergency telephone number
- The proper action to take if an incident using a particular chemical were to occur
- Direction for safe handling and use

Figure 4.4: COSHH symbols

Website: For more information visit the COSHH website http://www.hse.gov.uk/coshh/index.htm

4.6 Personal Protective Equipment at Work Regulations 1992 (protective clothing) 'PPE'

PPE legislation requires that employers provide the correct *work wear* to employees to reduce any accidents in the workplace.

The Health and Safety Executive details "PPE is defined in the Regulations as 'all equipment (including clothing affording protection against the weather) which is intended to be worn or held by a person at work and which protects him against one or more risks to his health or safety', eg safety helmets, gloves, eye protection, high-visibility clothing, safety footwear and safety harnesses".

A C T I V I T Y   2   5   m i n u t e s

What types of protective clothing would be required for Housekeeping personnel and in carrying out what types of tasks would it be required?

4.7 The Reporting of Injuries, Diseases and Dangerous Occurrences Regulations 1995 (RIDDOR)

RIDDOR is the law that states that all establishments must **record any accidents or ill health** that occur within the workplace (this could be accidents concerning employees, customers or visitors).

Why should I report?

- Reporting accidents and ill health at work is a legal requirement. The information enables the Health and Safety Executive (HSE) and local authorities, to identify where and how risks arise, and to investigate serious accidents. The authorities can then help and provide advice on how to reduce injury, and ill health in your workplace.

What should I document?

- You must keep a record of any reportable injury, disease or dangerous occurrence. This must include the date and method of reporting; the date, time and place of the event; personal details of those involved; and a brief description of the nature of the event or disease.

4.8 First-aid regulations 1981

Legal duties

- The Health and Safety (First-Aid) Regulations 1981 require employers to provide adequate and appropriate equipment, facilities and personnel to enable first-aid to be given to employees if they are injured or become ill at work. These Regulations apply to all workplaces including those with five or fewer employees and to the self-employed.

Assessment of first-aid needs

- Employers are required to carry out an assessment of first-aid needs. This involves consideration of workplace hazards and risks, the size of the organisation and other relevant factors, to determine what first aid equipment, facilities and personnel should be provided.

  Web site: http://www.hse.gov.uk/firstaid/index.htm

A C T I V I T Y   3   2 0   m i n u t e s

Speak with your facilities manager within your college, school or workplace and investigate what first-aid procedures are put in place to deal with accidents.

ACTIVITY 4   45 minutes

How would a manager deal with and treat the following accidents?

- A laundry worker burning himself on a hot steam iron

- A room maid scalding herself with some boiling water

- An in-room customer feeling dizzy and faint

- A maid comes across a customer in the corridor who has recently collapsed and is gripping his/her chest

- A housekeeping porter has cut his hand badly when closing a door

ACTIVITY 5   15 minutes

What medical supplies would need to be stocked in a Housekeeping department's first aid box?

4.9   Fire

The risk of fires starting in hotels needs to be taken seriously by hotel operators and managers. Fires can start in various ways and can include:

- Faulty equipment
- Faulty electrical wiring
- Smoking
- Exposed flames
- Overheating of electric or gas heaters
- Electric blankets
- Incorrect mixing of chemicals
- Blocked stairways
- Accumulated rubbish

The Fire Precautions Act of 1971

- Any premises used as a place of work, or to which members of the general public have access need to have a **valid fire certificate** issued by the fire authority.

- The fire authority must be satisfied that the **means of escape** in the event of fire, means of fire-fighting and means of giving warning are adequate.

- Particulars of any highly flammable, or explosive materials need to be recorded.

- The Act also covers the **training of people of 'what to do' in the event of fire**.

- It also gives the fire authority the right to inspect any premises to ascertain if there have been any changes in conditions, as any changes require a new fire certificate.

Fire extinguishers

All establishments must provide a selection of fire extinguishers to deal with each type of fire. These should be:

- Positioned strategically around the building and each department
- Correctly labelled
- Full
- Have a recent check certificate

Illustrated below are the different types of extinguishers and their uses.

BPP
LEARNING MEDIA

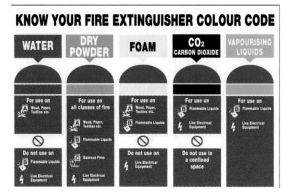

Figure 4.5: Fire extinguishers

FOR DISCUSSION

What other types of fire equipment you would find in a hotel?

Common fire safety features

- Smoke detectors in rooms and areas throughout hotel
- Self-closing doors
- Water sprinklers
- Fire extinguishers
- Fire alarms
- Fire doors
- Emergency lighting
- Hotel evacuation signs

ACTIVITY 6   20 minutes

As part of the new employee induction, the Human resources officer has asked you to get into groups and research what employees should do on discovering a fire. Using the internet or books, write down the main things employees should do on discovering a fire.

4.10   Safety Signs and Signals Regulations 1996

HSE explains 'The regulations bring into force an EC directive encouraging the standardisation of safety signs. These include the use of illuminated signs, hand and acoustic signals (eg fire alarms), spoken communication and the marking of pipework containing dangerous substances. These are in addition to traditional signboards such as prohibition and warning signs. Fire safety signs (ie signs for fire exits and fire-fighting equipment) are also covered'.

Requirements

- Employers must maintain safety signs
- Employers need to explain unfamiliar signs to employees
- Signs used need to meet the requirements of the regulations

Signs Regulations 1992

Figure 4.6: Sign regulations

A C T I V I T Y   7   **5   m i n u t e s**

How many of the signs can you identify in Figure 4.6?

5   Risk assessment

Source: http://www.lancall.co.uk

5.1   What is a risk?

- The chance, high, or low, that someone might be harmed by a hazard, experiencing danger, loss or injury.

5.2   What is a hazard?

- Hazards can either be acute or chronic risk. Acute is short-term and chronic is long-term. An example of an acute hazard may be an electric shock whereby a chronic hazard may be skin problems after many years of using cleaning chemicals.

Organisations are now required by law to carry out an assessment of risks within their operation.

5.3   Requirements

- Every employer must make a suitable and sufficient assessment of the risks to the health and safety of employees while at work; and the risks to the health and safety of people who are not employees, but who may be affected by the employer's operations.

- Risk assessments to be reviewed and amended to reflect changes in operations. For example, when there is reason to suspect that the risk assessment is no longer valid because a particular task is no longer carried out or the task is done in a different way, or a new task is implemented. If changes are required following a review, the employer must enforce them.

- Specific risk assessments to be carried out for young people and new or expectant mothers.

- Recording of significant findings of the risk assessment (if the business has five or more employees) and identifying any group of employees who are shown to be especially at risk. Recording includes publishing the assessment and bringing it to the attention of all employees.

There are **five** steps to risk assessment

- Step 1 – **Look for the hazards**.

- Step 2 – **Decide who might be harmed and how**.

- Step 3 – **Evaluate the risks** and decide whether the existing precautions are adequate or whether more should be done. (Risk is a combination of the hazard and the frequency with which a person is exposed to it. In evaluating the risk, the effectiveness of controls needs to be considered).

- Step 4 – **Record your findings** (a record of preventative and protective measures in place to control the risks and a register of any further action needed to control the risk to prove that a suitable and sufficient assessment has been made).

- Step 5 – **Review** your assessment and revise if necessary. (The level of detail in the risk assessment should be proportionate to the risk. The risks depend on the size of the organisation Employers are expected to refer to guidance and trade association publications to assist in identifying the risks. Records of risk assessments should include a note as to how long they remain valid).

Note: The person undertaking the risk assessment should be 'competent', that is, have appropriate training and experience.

ACTIVITY 8   30 minutes

You are Housekeeping supervisor and responsible for preparing a training session in Health and Safety for room attendants within the Housekeeping department. What five areas would you address? Explain reasons for their importance.

ACTIVITY 9   60 minutes

As a room-cleaning attendant how would you deal with the following situations for an occupied room?

- You discover a customer smoking in a non-smoking room.

- You see smoke coming from under a bedroom door.

- The guest is doing his own laundry and drying it on the in-room heaters.

- You see a colleague slip while cleaning inside a bathroom.

- You have come across a customer who has cut herself on a broken glass.

- A customer has slipped in the main lobby, but appears to be ok.

- You are unsure how to use a particular chemical.

- A customer whose room you have been cleaning for a few days is making you feel nervous and uncomfortable.

- A guest enters the room while you are cleaning it and informs you that it is his room and he has forgotten something.

- You are suffering from work stress due to too heavy a work load.

6 Hotel leisure facilities

6.1 Health and Safety considerations

Most hotels nowadays provide some form of leisure or recreation facility for its residents and non-residents.

However, the majority of these facilities are now outsourced to specialised contractors. These contractors are proficient in all areas of leisure management and health and safety.

Leisure facilities can include:

Hotel operators need to ensure that these facilities are kept clean and hygienic and that all safety guidelines are enforced to minimise risk to customers and employees.

As with other areas the same legal regulations apply, such as risk assessment, COSHH, RIDDOR, first-aid, MSDS, PPE and manual handling. Crisis planning is another important consideration for this area.

6.2 Swimming pools

Hotel responsibility

- No pool accidents
- Minimise the spread of disease and contamination
- Correct use of chemicals and exact chemical balance

No pool accidents

- Provision of qualified lifeguards
- Correct quantity of lifeguards per amount of swimmers
- If lifeguards not provided clear rules on minimum age of swimmer and parental supervision
- While in water supervisor to accompany minor at all times
- Availability of qualified first-aiders on staff
- Clear, well positioned warning signs
- Readily available life-saving equipment – rings, ropes and shepherd's hooks
- Lane dividers during sessions
- Restrictions on objects brought into pool
- Depth measurements clearly displayed
- Safety fences
- Deal with any wet areas around pool to reduce slipping
- No glass or china in pool area (plastic only)
- All broken tiles, cracks to be reported to Maintenance promptly
- Pool temperatures to be displayed
- When pool not in use, area must be securely locked to prevent unauthorised access

Source: http://www.cheappoolproducts.com

Minimise the spread of disease and contamination

Hotels need to enforce rules to reduce the opportunity of the spread of disease, therefore:

- Showering before entering the pool
- No swimmers permitted with skin, ear or eye infections
- Always leave pool to use toilet facility
- Ensure babies wear tight fitting nappies
- Do not swim shortly after consuming food
- No consuming foods while swimming

Correct use of chemicals and exact chemical balance

Pool and spa water must be monitored to ensure that it is safe for people to swim or sit in it. Possibility that bacteriologically unsafe or chemical concentrations may be too high.

- Follow COSHH guidelines (correct mixing, read labels, correct storage)
- Use MSDS sheets
- Clean-up any chemical spillages promptly
- Use suggested safety clothing
- Maintain chemical and temperature records
- Daily readings
- Pool testing at least three times per day

Main tests for pool water

1. Residual disinfectant and disinfectant by-products (free & combined chlorine)
2. Water balance (ph, total alkalinity, calcium hardness, temperature)
3. Undesirable residual chemicals (sulphates, chlorides, cyanurates)

6.3 Gymnasium

Gym equipment as indicated below poses many risks to users.

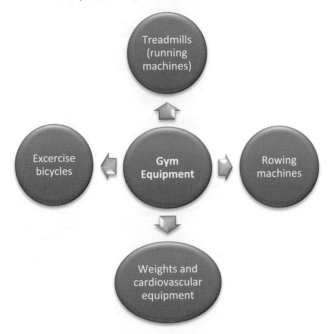

Hotel responsibilities

- To provide qualified gym personnel
- Screen users for current health status (or use warning signs)
- Instructors to ensure users are conversant with use of gym equipment
- To monitor guests use of equipment
- To check equipment daily for serviceability and safety
- Report any equipment defects promptly to Maintenance and put out of order
- Provision of cleaning equipment for daily cleaning

6.4 Sauna safety

Source: http://www.bleiglass.com

Hotel responsibilities

- Maintain cleanliness
- Clear signage with regard to supervision of minors
- Provision of emergency button
- Provide clear display of any relevant health warnings
- Ongoing monitoring of temperature by employees

6.5 Solarium (sun tanning) safety

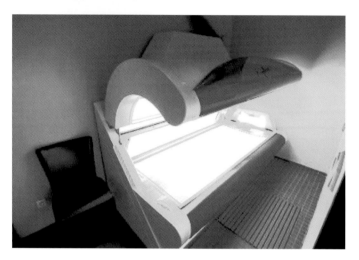

Source: http://prague.corinthia.cz

Hotel responsibilities

- Provide clean facilities (clean after each use)
- Inform of health risks
- Provide eye goggles
- Advise only ten minutes per session

SUMMARY

SELF-TEST QUESTIONS

1 List three ways to prevent fires.

2 Explain what is meant by the Data Protection Act 1998.

3 List three actions that managers can take to reduce employee work stress.

4 Which legislation is associated with the lifting or moving of heavy loads or equipment?

5 Give some examples of how organisations can make their office workspaces more ergonomic.

6 What does COSHH stand for?

7 Explain what is meant by RIDDOR and provide an example.

8 List three ways in which hotels can fulfil first-aid requirements.

9 A water-based fire extinguisher should not be used on which type of fires?

10 Explain the five steps of conducting a risk assessment.

SELF-TEST ANSWERS

1 Internal fire detection system, sprinklers/fire evacuation notices/fire marshals/fire extinguishers

2 That organisations must protect customers' personal data

3 Good scheduling. Regular breaks, job chats, fair distribution and allocation of work, observation and MBWA

4 Manual Handling Regulations 1992

5 Adjustable chairs and desks, VDU screen covers, wrist rests

6 Control of Substances Hazardous to Health

7 RIDDOR means that if accidents occur in the workplace the organisation has a legal responsibility to record that accident

8 First-aid boxes, first-aid training, first-aiders

9 On electrical fires

10 Look for the hazards, decide who is at risk, evaluate, record and review

ANSWERS TO ACTIVITIES

1

Group	Health risks
Hotel customers	▪ Fire
	▪ Pests/infestation
	▪ Trips and falls
	▪ Pollution
	▪ Faulty equipment
	▪ Electrical/maintenance defects
	▪ Contamination
	▪ Burns and scalds
	▪ Burglary/theft
	▪ Food poisoning
	▪ Harassment from other customers
	▪ Terrorist attacks
	▪ At risk from hotel employees
	▪ Threat of attacks from other customers
	▪ Theft of assets/personal data
	▪ Suspicious packages
	▪ Internal fraudulent practices

Housekeeping employees	▪ Back problems
	▪ Defective equipment
	▪ Contamination from needles
	▪ Stress – workload
	▪ Harassment from customers
	▪ Equipment flexes
	▪ Faulty electrics
	▪ Broken glass
	▪ Lifting
	▪ Ladder work
	▪ Wet floors
	▪ High floors and balconies
	▪ Allergies to chemicals
	▪ Dangerous chemicals

2 Flat shoes – All Personnel

Gloves – Chemicals

Gloves – Blood-stained linen

3 This answer depends on personal research.

4

Accident	Action
A laundry worker burning himself on a hot steam iron	Turn off machine
	Run cold water over burn to reduce swelling
	Apply burn cream from first aid box
	Cover with bandage
	Allow employee to rest
	Record in accident book
	Further training to prevent
A room maid scalding herself with some boiling water	Run cold water over burn to reduce swelling
	Apply burn cream from first aid box
	Cover with bandage
	Allow employee to rest
	Record in accident book/log incident
	Further training to prevent
An in-room customer feeling dizzy and faint	Open doors and vents
	Call first aider
	Make customer comfortable
	Follow up later with customer that all is OK
	Report in accident book/log incident

A maid comes across a customer in the corridor who has recently collapsed and is gripping his/her chest	Remain calm
	Call operator to call ambulance
	Call first aider
	Stay with customer
	Escort customer to hospital
	Notify relatives
	Record in accident book/log incident
A housekeeping porter has cut his hand badly when closing a door	Sit down employee
	Call first aider
	Apply first aid/bandage
	Report in accident book
	Clean any blood/spillage
	Allow employee to rest

5
- Burn gel
- Blue plasters
- Bandage

6
- Remain calm
- Fight the fire only if you have been trained and it is safe to do so
- Activate the nearest fire alarm
- Assist customers to leave the building through dedicated fire exits
- Leave the building by the nearest available exit (not the lift)
- Go to the hotel fire assembly point

7
Top row, left to right: no access, headgear required, no smoking

Bottom row, left to right: toxic, corrosive, flammable

8
Could include
- Lifting correctly – preventing back strain
- Using chemicals – avoiding contamination
- Reaching – avoiding muscle strain and injury
- Dealing with sharps (needles) – avoiding contamination; being aware of correct disposal techniques
- Safe disposal of glass – preventing cuts
- Using ladders for high dusting – height safety
- Pushing trolleys – preventing muscle strain
- Cleaning bath tiles and standing safely in the bath tub – avoiding slips and injuries

9

You discover a customer smoking in a non-smoking room.	Politely ask the customer to stop, and inform them of the regulations
	Inform duty manager and monitor
You see smoke coming from under a bedroom door.	Remain calm
	Pull the fire alarm
	Follow hotel fire instructions

The guest is doing his own laundry and drying it on the in-room heaters.	Inform customer that this is a fire risk and remove it
	Inform customer that hotel can organise drying of clothes in laundry if required
You see a colleague slip while cleaning inside a bathroom.	Assist
	Alert first aider if required
	Record in accident book
	Allow employee to rest
You have come across a customer who has cut herself on a broken glass.	Assist
	Alert first aider if required
	Record in accident book
	Promptly clean up breakage
	Allow customer to rest
	Monitor and follow up with customer throughout the day
A customer has slipped in the main lobby, but appears to be OK.	Assist
	Alert first aider if required
	Record in accident book
	Allow customer to rest
	Monitor and follow up with customer throughout the day
	Consider if there is a trip hazard
You are unsure how to use a particular chemical.	Either:
	Read label, or
	Contact supervisor for guidance
	Follow performance standard if available
A customer whose room you have been cleaning for a few days is making you feel nervous and uncomfortable.	Notify manager and explain
A guest enters the room while you are cleaning it and informs you that it is his room and he has forgotten something.	Ask to see room key
	If no room key ask to go to reception
	No entry to anyone unauthorised
You are suffering from work stress due to too heavy a work load.	Inform manager

CHAPTER 5

LINEN ROOM AND LAUNDRY

Chapter objectives

By the end of this chapter you will be able to

- Explain the different types of linen, their strengths and weaknesses
- Describe the considerations when selecting and purchasing linen
- Present the linen cycle and explain the key quality and financial considerations at each stage
- Discuss the function of a linen room, its equipment and systems
- Define different strategies to maintain linen stocks

Topic list
Types of linen
Selecting and purchasing linen
The linen cycle
The control of linen

'Linen is the most important recycled inventory item under the executive housekeeper's responsibility. Next to personnel, linen costs are the highest expense in the housekeeping department'.

Kappa et al. (1997)

1 Types of linen

- Fabrics are manufactured from fibres which may be woven, knitted, or bonded together in various ways.

- Different fabrics have different properties making them appropriate for use in varying situations.

- All fabrics are collectively called 'linen' in hospitality jargon, even though the material may be made of fibres other than linen. Linen can be classified as the following types.

Bed linen	Bathroom linen	Table linen (Food and Beverage)	Other
Bed sheets	Face towels	Napkins	Cushion covers
Pillow cases	Hand towels	Table cloths	Loose covers
Blankets	Bath towels	Slip cloths	Curtains/drapes
Bedspreads	Bath mats	Table skirting	Blinds
Mattress protector	Bathrobe	Underlays	Shades
Duvet covers	Shower curtains	Chair slips	
Electric blankets		Conference baize	
Quilts			
Slippers			

ACTIVITY 1   60 minutes

Find pictures of the linen types as given above.

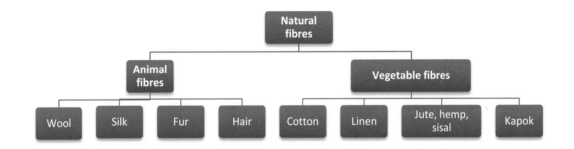

Figure 5.1: Natural fibres

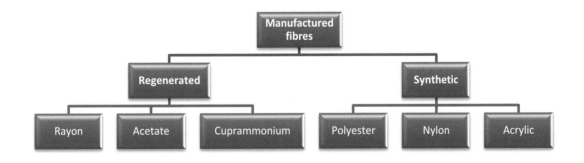

Figure 5.2: Manufactured fibres

DEFINITION

Cuprammonium – a method of producing a type of regenerated rayon fibre.

ACTIVITY 2   20 minutes

How many of the fibres illustrated in Figures 5.1 and 5.2 do you have in your home?

Fibre	Advantages	Disadvantages	Uses
Cotton (manufactured from the seed of the cotton plant)	Strong, good absorbency, stronger when wet, can be starched, can be washed and ironed at high temperatures	Some shrinkage (5-15% on first wash). Low colour retention.	Bed linen, **soft furnishings**, uniforms, napkins
Wool (fibres, usually from sheep)	Good insulation	Does not wash well, felts, not durable, becomes weak when wet, shrinks and mats, very absorbent and does not last long with industrial cleaning.	Blankets, carpets, baize (to cover boardroom tables), uniforms, upholstery, curtains
Linen (manufactured from the stem of the flax plant)	Very luxurious fabric. Very good dirt and abrasion resistant qualities	Has little resilience and creases badly	Bed linen, soft furnishings, glass cloths, upholstery and table linen
Silk (manufactured from filaments spun by the cultivated silkworm)	Smooth, lustrous, elastic and resilient. Does not crush easily	Is fragile and disintegrates in sunlight and is weaker wet than dry	Curtains, wall coverings, bed linen, some uniform items
Jute, ramie, hemp, sisal (manufactured from the stems of the plants from which they are named)	All very strong and durable		Manufacture of carpets, backings for linoleum and for upholstery
Kapok (manufactured from the seeds of the kapok tree)	Very light, smooth and soft fibres		Used as fillings for cushions and pillows in upholstery, but largely superseded by foam or terylene
Regenerated fibres – rayon, cuprammonium, acetate (usually manufactured from regenerated cellulose (or pure cellulose in acetate)	Smooth, soft and lustrous fabrics (cuprammonium is like silk)	Can decompose or melt at high temperatures, vulnerable to chemicals. Can crease badly (viscose)	Can be used in furnishing fabrics, blankets, or curtains. May often be blended with other, stronger fabrics.

Fibre	Advantages	Disadvantages	Uses
Polyester (Terylene. Manufactured from petroleum products)	Good resistance to abrasion and sunlight	Low moisture absorption and can melt at high temperatures	Used as fillings for duvets, pillows. Can be used as bed linen, furnishing fabrics, uniforms and is often blended with cotton
Polyamide (Nylon. Originally manufactured from coal tar products, nowadays petroleum chemicals are used)	Easy to launder and dry, very durable, elastic and abrasion resistant	Melts at relatively low temperatures	Bed linens, furnishing fabrics, uniforms
Acrylic, eg dralon – manufactured from petroleum chemicals	Resembles wool and has a fluffy, warm and soft feel. Good resistance to sunlight and chemicals	Melts at high temperatures. Low moisture absorbency	Furnishings and upholstery fabrics, blankets and carpets.
Polypropylene (manufactured from petroleum chemicals)	Very good abrasion resistance and light in weight	Zero absorption	Twine, carpets

DEFINITION

Soft furnishings – furniture that is upholstered over padding, filling or stuffing. Examples include chairs, sofas, ottomans and stools.

Other types of soft furnishings can include large floor pillows, chaise longues and padded garden furniture.

1.1 Uses of linen and fabrics

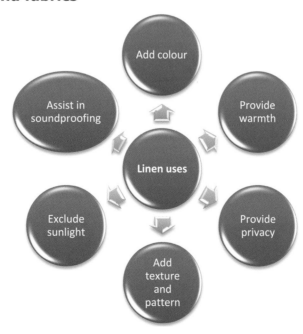

2   Selecting and purchasing linen

2.1   Considerations when selecting and purchasing linen

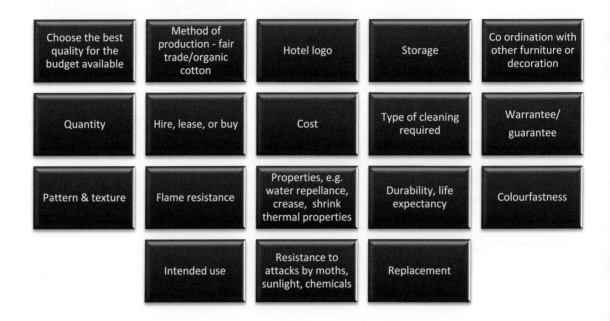

Choose the best quality for the budget available	Method of production - fair trade/organic cotton	Hotel logo	Storage	Co ordination with other furniture or decoration
Quantity	Hire, lease, or buy	Cost	Type of cleaning required	Warrantee/ guarantee
Pattern & texture	Flame resistance	Properties, e.g. water repellance, crease, shrink thermal properties	Durability, life expectancy	Colourfastness
	Intended use	Resistance to attacks by moths, sunlight, chemicals	Replacement	

ACTIVITY 3   **45 minutes**

You are the executive housekeeper for a new hotel and you have the responsibility for equipping the hotel with all its linen. If the hotel has 240 standard rooms, how many towels would you order for its bedrooms? Is there any specific formula? What you would need to consider?

3   The linen cycle

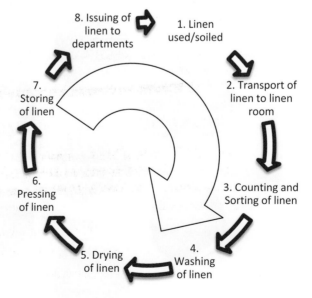

Figure 5.3: The Linen Cycle

The linen cycle (see Figure 5.3) details the movement of linen throughout the hotel. Most linen will go through this process, however, it can change with regard to:

- The length of time (turnaround time) from linen being soiled to it being cleaned
- Whether the cleaning is carried out within the hotel or contracted out to an external laundry
- The methods of cleaning used

Dealing with laundry is a fact of life for hotels. Guest rooms, restaurants, banquets, fitness centres and employees all have soiled linens: towels, tablecloths, uniforms and other laundry that must be cleaned. Hotels have several choices in how they handle this, they can:

- Use disposable products where possible (paper rather than linen napkins, for example)
- Rent clean linens from a commercial laundry
- Buy their own linens from a commercial laundry
- Buy their own linens and use a commercial laundry
- Buy their own linens and use a centralised laundry
- Buy their own linens and use an on premise laundry
- Use a combination of these alternatives

Stipanuk and Roffmann (1996)

3.1 Internal laundry

When considering the set-up of an internal laundry the following factors would have to be considered:

- Location
- Space – what would determine how much space you need?
- Accessibility
- Lighting and ventilation
- Staffing
- Training
- Equipment
- Health and Safety
- Drainage
- Operating costs
- Business forecast
- Control
- Guest laundry
- Uniforms
- Supervision
- Quality control procedures

3.2 Laundry 'own or contract'?

It is very common nowadays for hotels to send out their laundry to a specialised laundry contractor.

	Advantages	Disadvantages
Own laundry in-house	■ More control in the areas of quality, supervision ■ Faster **turnaround**	■ Occupies valuable space ■ Capital investment in equipment ■ Equipment – maintenance, repair, training and depreciation ■ Utility expense (gas, electricity, water) ■ Labour costs – recruitment, training, benefits ■ Chemical costs

External laundry	• Only pay for what you require laundered	• Lead time – time taken from leaving hotel to return
	• No fixed or variable costs	• Potential lack of control
	• Pass on responsibility	• Potential loss of linen
	• Use space to generate revenue (outsource to other retailers, hairdressers, tailors etc)	• Difficult to compile inventory
		• Difficult to control lifespan
	• Greater specialisation	
	• Concentrate focus on other areas	

Turnaround – the total time required for the linen to complete the linen cycle.

DEFINITION

FOR DISCUSSION

Are internal laundries better for the organisation and the customer?

FOR DISCUSSION

Is using an external laundry cheaper for hotels?

3.3 The linen cycle steps

As illustrated in Figure 5.3 the linen cycle has eight steps. At each stage the executive housekeeper has to maintain both focus on **financial and quality control**.

Step 1 – use of linen/soiled linen

Each bedroom has a par level of linen. For example, one standard room usually has the following linen for each bathroom:

- 2 bath towels
- 2 face towels
- 2 hand towels

When customers occupy the room they either:

- Use the bath linen and have fresh linen replaced
- Reuse the same towels throughout the duration of their stay

A recent trend is for hotels to display signs to promote the reuse of linen. For example, if a customer is concerned about the environment and is staying a few days they can reuse the same towels, just like at home. The benefits of this are that less laundry is cleaned which is good for the environment, the hotel saves money and the customer feels good. However, in most cases the used linen will be replaced with fresh.

Step 2 – transport of linen to linen room

Throughout the day the room attendants collect a lot of soiled linen which is placed into a laundry bin or trolley. This linen is then transported to the linen room by Housekeeping porters. In some hotels linen is simply bundled and deposited by means of a linen chute.

3.4 The linen room

Figure 5.4: Main responsibilities of the linen/laundry room

Step 3 – counting and sorting of linen

On arrival at the linen room the laundry room attendant will:

- Count each piece of linen.

- Separate linens into size, type and colour.

- Check for any damaged or heavily soiled item (damaged linen is removed from the operation and heavily soiled linen treated separately, as given below).

- In some cases the same amount of clean linen stock is given back to the attendant.

- Each floor has their own pantry which contains a **par level stock** of linen, a sufficient quantity to replenish all rooms. This stock is put onto the room attendants' trolleys in the morning in preparation to put into the bedrooms. The system of 'clean for dirty' linen makes room attendants more accountable for the retention of their linen stock. If they are asking for more stock than they have deposited, why is this?

- At this stage the laundry is either collected and sent to an external laundry contractor or washed in-house.

Par level – the standard quantity of each item that must be available to support the housekeeping operation. Par levels are created by considering different factors such as the demand of the item, and storage space available.

DEFINITION

EXAMPLE

Below is a list of items and their par stock levels for a housekeeper's pantry.

Item	Par level	Min	Max
Bath towel	30	20	40
Face towel	30	20	40
Pillow case	80	40	90
Bed sheet	40	20	50

Minimal par level is what the stock must never go below and similarly the maximum is what must not be exceeded. When stock is removed, new stock needs to be requested to bring the stock back up to the par level.

Type of staining	Method of removal
Red wine	Use a clean dry cloth, then add cold water and blot up the area. Can also use a specific stain remover or baking soda.
Blood	Hydrogen peroxide or shaving cream for linen
Candle wax	Brown paper and a hot iron
Grease	Warm water and detergent
Lipstick	Shaving foam, soda, glycerine

ACTIVITY 4   45 minutes

How should the stains listed below be removed from linen or laundry items?

Stain	Method of removal?
Chewing gum	
Ink	
Blood	
Grease	
Coffee	
Candle wax	
Mildew	

Step 4 – washing of linen

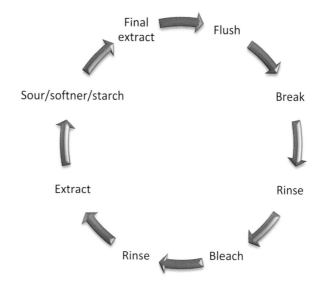

Figure 5.5: The wash cycle

At the washing stage there are particular things that need to be carried out to maintain quality and cost control.

When loading, the machines should not be too empty or too full and the operator should:

- Ensure the correct laundry chemical is used and the right quantity for the load/weight
- Ensure the wash temperature is correct
- Ensure colours are not mixed

Many large machines nowadays are computerised and the chemical quantity and washing temperatures are calculated automatically.

A C T I V I T Y 5   **3 0 m i n u t e s**

What would be some of the impacts of not following the above guidelines when washing laundry?

Source: http://www.infinitycleaning.co.uk

Figure 5.6: Industrial washers

Step 5 – drying linen

After washing, in most cases, the laundry is dried in large commercial dryers. Again, during this stage quality and financial considerations must be followed, to include that the:

- Machine should not be too full or too empty
- Machine drying temperature should not be too hot or too cold
- Drying time should be correct for the laundry load, not too short or too long

Similarly, computerised dryers now calculate the time and temperature required based on the load/weight.

Step 6 – pressing and folding

For linen to be crisp and appear professionally laundered the next stage is for it to be pressed. Laundries have different ways of doing this to include:

- Steam cabinets
- Flatwork ironers
- Pressing machines
- Folding machines
- Rolling equipment

Source: http://www.tingue.com

Figure 5.7: Linen/laundry room employees operating a 'flatwork ironer'

Step 7 – storing linen

After folding, the linen will be stored. The main linen room will have a par stock level for all linen items to ensure that the hotel has sufficient quantities of linen at any one time to accommodate the needs of the departments.

The linen should **rest** in storage for at least 24 hours before being issued. This helps increase the useful life of linens and makes the linen smoother. The linen rooms need adequate ventilation, be humidity-free and lockable.

Step 8 – issuing linen

Linen is issued from the linen room to Housekeeping porters, room attendants and other departments throughout the day. Most linen rooms practice some form of control at this stage, such as employees signing for any linen types and quantities received. Other hotels may have a system whereby Housekeeping porters and room attendants restock their linen pantries as and when required. The important element is tracking who has taken what linen and to which area.

ACTIVITY 6   **15 minutes**

Many hotel food and beverage outlets use very little linen to reduce their operating expenses. Give three ways in which this can be done.

4   The control of linen

Linen is a hotel asset and needs to be controlled and this is one of the main functions of the executive housekeeper, ensuring the linen stock level is maintained. When linen stocks reduce this is referred to as 'shrinkage' and can occur due to:

- Employee misuse
- Poor treatment, washing and drying methods
- Misplaced in external laundry
- Customer or employee theft

Some methods adopted by hotels to control shrinkage are given below.

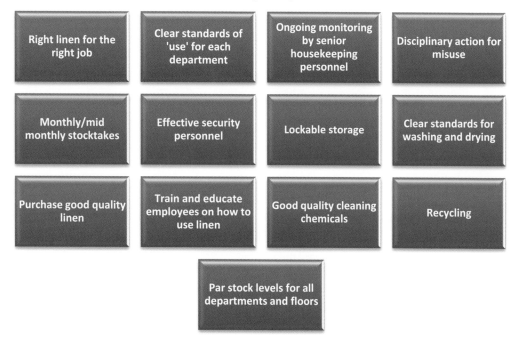

Right linen for the right job	Clear standards of 'use' for each department	Ongoing monitoring by senior housekeeping personnel	Disciplinary action for misuse
Monthly/mid monthly stocktakes	Effective security personnel	Lockable storage	Clear standards for washing and drying
Purchase good quality linen	Train and educate employees on how to use linen	Good quality cleaning chemicals	Recycling
	Par stock levels for all departments and floors		

BPP LEARNING MEDIA

ACTIVITY 7   45 minutes

The table below presents a quick snapshot of the results for a typical monthly linen stocktake.

- What conclusions can be drawn from the results?
- What would the possible causes be for any shortfalls?
- What recommendations can you suggest for any improvements?

	Unit cost	Count end of last month	Discards	Purchases	Count end of this month
White bath towel	£7.00	2200	12	0	1950
White face towel	£2.25	2457	0	0	2455
White hand towel	£2.25	2933	0	0	2961
Bed sheet (king size)	£12.00	1450	3	0	1447
Bed sheet (queen size)	£11.00	1377	0	0	1396
Food and Beverage table napkin (pink)	£12.00	1906	20	0	1735

ACTIVITY 8   20 minutes

Visit the home furnishings section within a large, local department store. View the towels and bedding display and give details of:

- Their origin, where were they made?
- Their production, how were they made?
- Their quality?
- Washing guidelines.

DEFINITION

Discards – linen items that no longer meet the required standard. For example, towels that have frayed edges or stained bed linen.

Hotels commonly think of creative ways to re-use their discarded items. For example, old bed sheets may be used to cover ironing boards, or cut up and used as cleaning cloths.

BPP LEARNING MEDIA

SUMMARY

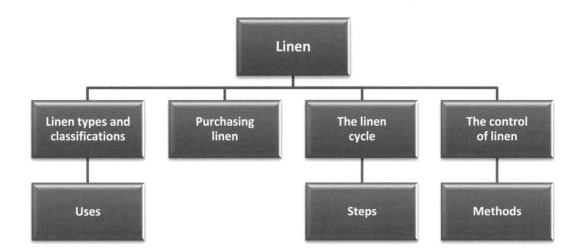

SELF-TEST QUESTIONS

1 Provide two examples of table linen.

2 Is kapok a vegetable or animal fibre?

3 Name some advantages for 'cotton' as a fabric.

4 Name two advantages for a hotel of having its own laundry.

5 Name the fifth step in the linen cycle.

6 Shaving foam, soda or glycerine would be used to remove which type of stain?

7 How long should linen rest for before reuse?

8 Name any five ways to control linen.

9 What is meant by the term linen 'shrinkage'?

10 How frequently should a linen inventory be carried out?

SELF-TEST ANSWERS

1   Tablecloths, napkins, slip cloths, underlay

2   Vegetable

3   Strong, good absorbency, stronger when wet, can be starched, can be washed and ironed at high temperatures

4   More control in the areas of quality, supervision, faster turnaround

5   Drying

6   Lipstick

7   24 hours

8   Any answer as detailed in section 4

9   Shrinkage is the reduction of linen stocks

10   Monthly or twice monthly

ANSWERS TO ACTIVITIES

1 The answer to this activity depends on personal research.

2 The answer to this activity depends on personal research.

3 Need to consider the following:

- Total rooms
- Par level per room
- Turnaround time from dirty to clean
- Estimated loss
- Emergency stock

For example 240 rooms x 2 towels per room = 480

3 days for cleaning = 1,440

+ 10 loss per month = 120

+ 100 emergency stock

= 1,660

Note: When outsourcing laundry of linen, some contracts will provide linen itself, which eliminates the capital investment in linen by the hotel.

4

Stain	Method of removal
Chewing gum	Hot water, leave for a few minutes, then remove with hard brush.
Ink	Use ink eradicator. Hold stain against towel, spray closely from behind with aerosol hair spray. Ink should transfer to towel
Blood	Immediately rinse with cool water. For dried stains, soak in warm water with a product containing enzymes. Launder.
Grease	Pre-treat with pre-wash stain remover or liquid laundry detergent. For heavy stains, place stain face down on clean paper towels. Apply cleaning agent to back of stain. Replace paper towels under stain frequently. Let dry, rinse and launder using hottest water safe for fabric.
Coffee	Stretch fabric tautly over a bowl and pour boiling water from high above.
Candle wax	Scrape off as much as possible with dull side of knife, then iron between absorbent paper, changing paper until wax is absorbed.
Mildew	Badly mildewed fabrics may be beyond repair. Launder stained item using chlorine bleach (if safe for fabric). Or soak in oxygen bleach and hot water. Then launder.

5

Action	Impact
Ensure the correct laundry chemical is used and the right quantity for the load/weight	If chemical is not correct it may damage the laundry. If the load is too much then maybe the laundry will not clean fully and will require further laundering
Ensure the wash temperature is correct	Too cold and it may not clean sufficiently, too hot on certain fabrics can cause shrinkage
Ensure colours are not mixed	Mixing coloured fabrics may result in colour mixing and damage presentation of colour

6
- No linen place mats
- Paper napkins
- Table cloths replaced by plastic covers or nice wooden table tops

7   **What conclusions can be drawn from the results?**

The linen stock is shrinking (reducing), which equates to a financial loss

What would the possible causes be for any shortfalls?

- Theft
- Incorrect stocktaking
- Damage leading to discards
- Lost in laundry or external laundry

What recommendations can you suggest for any improvements?

- Standards for conducting stocktakes
- Allocate chambermaids linen and make accountable for maintaining stock level
- Count linen going and returning from external laundry
- Standards for correct use of linen
- Standards for correct cleaning and drying of linen
- MBWA

8   The answer to this activity depends on personal research.

CHAPTER 6

MAINTENANCE AND THE ENVIRONMENT

Chapter objectives

By the end of this chapter you will be able to

- Explain the importance of good maintenance for customers, employees and the organisation
- Present strategies for effective maintenance quality control
- Discuss key positions within the department, their responsibilities and organisation
- Discuss the different types of maintenance and explain the main areas of responsibility for this department within the hotel
- Explain ways that hotels can be more environmentally friendly in their operations and towards the community

Topic list

Introduction to maintenance
Staffing and resources
Main areas of maintenance
Types of maintenance
The 'work order' system – day-to-day repairs
Environmental management in accommodation

Source: http://www.graham.co.uk

1   Introduction to maintenance

The Maintenance department's responsibilities include the upkeep of the overall appearance and working order of the hotel to incorporate guest rooms, public areas, common areas and the building exterior. Other duties include completing maintenance requests, conducting regular safety inspections and training staff on safety and security. Sometimes this department can also be referred to as 'Engineering' or 'Facilities'.

- The hospitality industry of today relies on well-designed and well-maintained facilities as a key element of its business.

- Facilities play a critical role in the money-making aspects of the business. They serve as a location for the delivery of services, play a role in estate appreciation and contribute to corporate growth.

Adapted from *Stipanuk and Roffman (1996)*

1.1   Objectives of the Maintenance department

- To maintain the hotel's internal and surrounding facilities
- To promptly repair any defective furniture, equipment or fittings
- Plan and oversee any major refurbishments, renovations or redecorations
- Contract external specialists to perform maintenance works as and when required
- To provide a safe, physical work environment for employees
- To provide safe premises for visitors and customers
- To actively work towards reducing energy costs

Maintenance is a major part of the hotel product. If the physical surroundings of the product are not maintained then this will affect the business. For an organisation to effectively sell its products all parts of the market mix have to be correct.

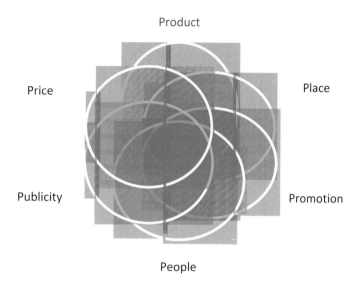

Figure 6.1: The market mix and its relationship to Maintenance and Facilities

Normally, the age of the product determines the amount of upkeep that is required. For example a new hotel would in most cases not require much maintenance. However, as the hotel ages its facilities start to deteriorate and require more frequent maintenance.

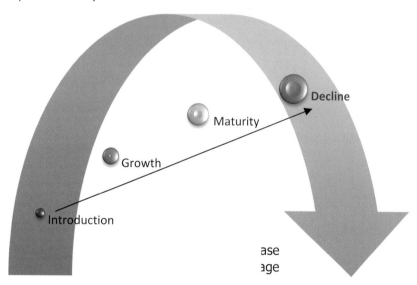

Figure 6.2: The product life cycle

Figure 6.3, below, highlights the importance linkage to products and how costs are incurred at each stage.

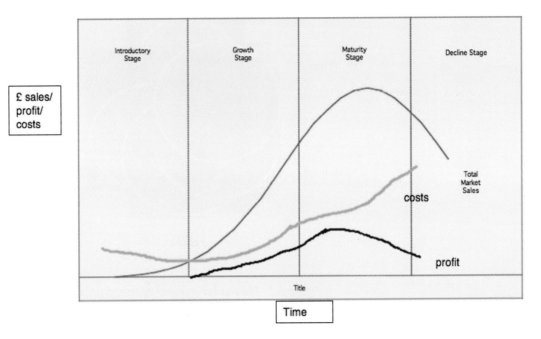

Figure 6.3: Costs and the product life cycle

Benefits of well-maintained facilities:

- More attractive
- Attracts and retains customers
- Remain competitive
- Safer environment for customers and employees
- Cost efficiency and reduction

The failure to maintain facilities can have many negative impacts as shown in the following diagram.

Figure: 6.4: Impacts of poor maintenance

To ensure that these impacts are minimised, different strategies need to be adopted, as shown below.

2 Staffing and resources

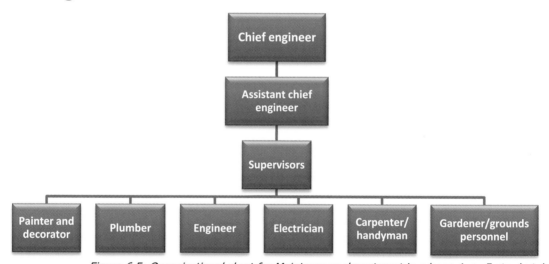

Figure 6.5: Organisational chart for Maintenance department in a large 4- or 5-star hotel

Very few hotels employ all of the specialised positions as detailed above. Most have general employees who work in the Maintenance department who may specialise in one area but also are cross-trained to carry out other maintenance tasks. For example, an employee who is a qualified plumber may have also had training on how to operate the energy management system. By cross-training employees greater flexibility is provided. Another approach is to have general handymen who can deal with everyday tasks but when a specialised piece of work needs to be done, a local contractor is employed, on an hourly rate, to carry out the work.

Due to the increase in technology many hotels now employ an IT technician to take care of all the hardware and software systems within the hotel.

Such systems may include:

- Property Management System (PMS)
- Point of Sale System (POS)
- Electronic Locking System (ELS)
- Energy Management System (EMS)

ACTIVITY 1   **5 minutes**

What types of hardware and software systems used are in different departments within large hotels?

2.1   Chief Engineer – job description

The Chief Engineer is an individual who is organised and reliable with attention to detail. The ideal candidate would be a team player, with a flexible approach, exceptional interpersonal and communication skills as well as great people management skills. The Chief Engineer will be able to handle all matters relating to the hotel's maintenance and repair.

Other skills that will need to be demonstrated include:

- Ability to prioritise and delegate when necessary
- Ability to maintain composure and multi-task while working under pressure
- Ability to maintain high standards of verbal and written communication in a pressurised environment
- Management skills
- Knowledge of preventative maintenance schemes
- Involvement in a refurbishment or restoration project desirable

Scope and purpose

As Chief Engineer, you will work alongside the Assistant Chief Engineer to oversee the efficient day-to-day running of the Technical Services department and you will supervise, motivate and organise the Technical Services team and the daily operations.

Your role will also involve assisting with all life safety systems such as the fire alarm, emergency lighting and gas detection systems.

You will have to understand and operate these systems with a level of in-house maintenance / breakdown response as well as control of external contractors / specialists to maintain the systems.

As Chief Engineer you will support the Assistant Chief Engineer and Technical Services department in assuming responsibility for keeping the hotel facilities in optimum operating condition, by performing preventative maintenance and repairs on hotel power plant machinery (including heat, power, air conditioning and refrigeration). As Chief Engineer you will follow the hotel and corporate policies and guidelines, and the hotel's business plan.

Main duties and responsibilities

- To support and ensure the Technical Services team carry out all general repairs and preventative maintenance of the guest bedrooms and front and back of house areas.

- To manage and support the Works Manager to ensure all PPM and general repairs are carried out in a timely and efficient manner.

- To oversee the day-to-day running of the department.

- To continuously endeavour to improve personal knowledge of the job.

- To ensure guest satisfaction by performing duties such as attending to their requests and enquiries courteously and efficiently and accepting changes or addition to work hours which are necessary for the maintenance of uninterrupted service to hotel guests and patrons.

- To keep adequate levels of supplies required for hotel maintenance and keep the stock of materials to an agreed level.

- To be an active member of the emergency team of the hotel.

- In conjunction with the Assistant Chief Engineer to ensure that the Engineering department is correctly staffed and trained with a suitable team for its function, and to ensure that these team members can perform their duties to the standard required by the hotel and the company.

- To monitor and supervise external contracting staff to ensure compliance with the house rules.

- To work with external contractors as necessary to assist them in performing maintenance or construction jobs.

The main responsibilities of a chief engineer include:

- The control of energy costs.

- The protection of the owner's investment.

- The creation of a working environment that results in the efficient operation of all departments.

- The operation of the maintenance area in a way that contributes positively to the guest experience.

- A continued attention to safety concerns related to the building, grounds, equipment and operational procedures.

- Contractual responsibility spelled out in management contracts and franchise agreements.

Stipanuk and Roffmann (1996)

3 Main areas of maintenance

	Examples
Plumbing and water systems	Central heating, boilers, spa, pool, sanitation, filtration, cleaning, irrigation, laundry, guest rooms, fountains, drainage
Electrical	Equipment, lighting, batteries, generators, meters, energy management
HVAC (heating, ventilation and air conditioning)	Temperatures, comfort, extraction, refrigeration, cooling systems, air supply
Lighting	Natural, in-room, public areas, task, emergency, exterior, colour, mood, ambience, decoration, energy saving
Laundry	Laundry equipment, energy management, wastewater
Telecommunication	Internet, switchboard (PABX), facsimile, intranet, Wifi, web site, e-mail, in-house pagers, mobile telephones
Safety and security	Signage, equipment, testing, electronic locking systems, alarm system, security lighting, parameter fences, fire system, sprinklers, CCTV, in-room safes, fingerprint recognition
Waste management	Recycling systems
Food service equipment	Kitchen equipment, refrigeration, ovens, buffet units, cook-chill units, storage, dishwasher, ice machines, coffee machines, vending machines
Energy management	Cost control, employees, customers, law, comfort, utility pricing
The building's exterior	Roof, walls, foundation, drainage, structure, sewers, water features, insulation, windows
Car park and grounds	Presentation, security, lighting, maintenance, irrigation, management and general upkeep
Design	Renovation, refurbishments, interior, comfort, fashion, health and safety, DDA

ACTIVITY 2   20 minutes

Carry out desk research on the following questions.

- What types of maintenance would be required in an in-house laundry?

- What is mean by a hotel 'PABX' system?

- List five benefits of an 'electronic locking system' (ELS) for a hotel.

- Detail ten pieces of equipment commonly found in commercial kitchens.

- List ten things that you would need to consider when designing a hotel bedroom.

Source: http://wb8.itrademarket.com

Figure 6.6: An example of an 'electronic locking system'

ACTIVITY 3   30 minutes

Energy conservation is a major part of the maintenance manager's role. Outline 20 strategies that you could adopt to reduce energy usage within hotels. Use the table at section 3, above, to assist with ideas, examples of which are given below.

- Use curtains to stop heat escaping
- Use energy-efficient light bulbs
- Switch off lights when not required
- Use rechargeable batteries
- Use rain water for irrigation

Websites

Visit the following websites to gain a better understanding and insight into energy management within hotels.

Marriott Hotels http://www.marriott.com/marriott.mi?page=environmentalInitiatives

ENERGY STAR™ http://www.energystar.gov/index.cfm?c=guidelines.guidelines_index

Calculate your personal environmental footprint:
www.conservation.org/act/live_green/carboncalc/Pages/default.aspx

4 Types of maintenance

Routine maintenance activities are those which relate to the general upkeep of the property, they occur on a regular (daily or weekly) basis, and require relatively minimal training or skills. They are maintenance tasks which occur outside of the formal work order system and which require no specific maintenance records (time or materials, examples include cleaning readily accessible windows, cutting grass, shovelling snow and replacing burned-out light bulbs.

Preventative maintenance consists of three parts: inspection, minor corrections and work order initiation. For many areas within the hotel, inspections are performed by Housekeeping personnel in the normal course of duties. For example, room attendants may regularly check guest rooms for leaking faucets, cracked caulking around bathroom fixtures and other items that may call for action by Engineering staff. Communication between Housekeeping and Engineering should be efficient so that most minor repairs can be handled while the room attendant is cleaning the guest room. In some properties, a full-time maintenance person may be assigned to inspect guest rooms and to perform the necessary repairs, adjustments, or replacements.

'Prevention is better than cure'

ACTIVITY 4   **30 minutes**

Create a spider diagram detailing the benefits of preventative maintenance for customers, employees and departmental expenses.

4.1 External contracted maintenance

Some maintenance requires **only** professional, **specialised** external contractors to repair or maintain facilities due to their complexity, such as:

- Lift/elevators
- Escalators
- Gas
- External window cleaning
- Pest control

4.2 Emergency maintenance

Emergency maintenance is when the maintenance is required **immediately**. This could be for example:

- Flooding
- Power cuts
- Leaking gas
- Explosions
- Structural faults
- System breakdowns

As highlighted by *Stipanuk and Roffmann (1996)* these forms of maintenance are particularly costly for the operation because:

- They are usually only solved with the application of premium pay (overtime).

- They often bypass the traditional parts or supplies purchasing system, leading to premium parts cost.

- They have other costs associated with their solution (for example, a leaking pipe may also damage walls and ceilings).

4.3 Renovations and refurbishments

DEFINITION

Stipanuk and Roffmann (1996) explain that 'Renovation is the process of renewing and updating a hospitality property'. Reasons to renovate:

- The furnishes and finishes within the facility are worn out

- The interior design is out-of-date and a source of embarrassment or is directly linked to declining revenues

- The market for the mix of facilities offered by the hotel has changed, and new opportunities are available only through renovating underutilised facilities to meet changing guest demands

- Present or previous ownership has spent the funds necessary to keep the hotel in a fully updated condition, and the physical plant has deteriorated. As a direct result, business volume has declined to a point where revenues do not support the hotel's level of debt

- Acquiring and renovating an existing hotel presents an opportunity that is superior to constructing a new hotel in terms of location, timing and costs

ACTIVITY 5   20 minutes

As an executive housekeeper what would you manage and who would you need to communicate with during a renovation/refurbishment process?

Scheduled maintenance activities are initiated at the property based on a formal work order system. Work orders are a key element in the communication between Housekeeping and Engineering.

Kappa et al. (1997)

5 The 'work order system' – day-to-day repairs

Throughout the hotel, in each department, repairs to furniture, fixtures and equipment are ongoing. To promptly rectify these defects most hospitality operations would use a 'work order' system, *sometimes referred to as a 'maintenance request'* as illustrated below in Figure 6.7.

EXAMPLE

A room attendant finds a broken table in a hotel bedroom. The hotel's agreement to customers is that it provides well-maintained facilities. Therefore the hotel needs to repair the table to ensure that customer satisfaction is achieved. Some repairs can affect the room being put out of order as it may be dangerous for customers to use (eg water temperature is too hot and unsafe). Similarly, if a room has a broken television it should not be sold as this is one of the main functions of the bedroom.

Whatever the defect, the problem needs to be resolved promptly and the work order system is a process of **documentation** and **communication** to get the defective item repaired quickly.

The employee completes a work form by detailing:

- Which department is recording the maintenance problem
- The employee reporting the problem
- The date and time of reporting
- A description of the problem
- The seriousness of the problem

This work order form is in 'triplicate' so the department reporting the problem keeps one copy of the request and the other two copies go to the Maintenance department (this may differ from hotel to hotel).

The Maintenance department manager then delegates the task to an employee on the Maintenance team. (See Figure 6.7).

The advantages of the work order system are:

- Written communication is traceable (verbally communicating defects can be forgotten).

- Triplicate copies allows for follow-up.

- Maintenance manager can use dockets to track departmental job costs.

- The maintenance manager can track workload and performance of each employee on the maintenance team.

- The maintenance manager can track performance of furniture, fixtures and equipment (FFEs).

- The maintenance manager uses these requests to build-up a history of defects per department.

Date: 17 May	Department: Housekeeping	Employee reporting Jane
Time: 1.22 pm	Location of maintenance problem Room 202	
Description of problem	Left side bedside table has cracked leg and is unstable.	
Very urgent	Somewhat urgent x	Not so urgent
Job allocated to 'employee name' Frank	Outcome: Table replaced. Cracked table leg repaired.	

Figure 6.7: Example of a 'work order'

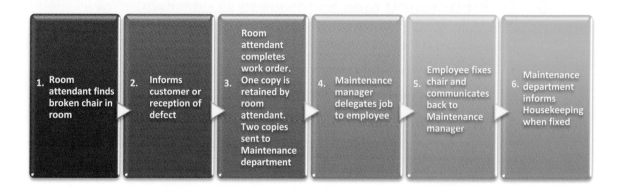

Figure 6.8: The work order process

Many hotels now use a computerised work order system to report faults. Employees simply enter the fault details into the computer and it links with the Maintenance and Reception departments. It allows departments to check the progress of any reported defects.

ACTIVITY 6   40 minutes

What would you consider to be common repairs/maintenance required in the following areas? Complete the table with your points.

Bedrooms	Food and Beverage and main kitchen	Leisure club and Spa	Public Areas	External Grounds
Examples: Leaking taps TV remote control not working	?	?	?	?

6 Environmental Management in accommodation

One of the most critical elements of becoming an environmentally friendly hotel is the adoption of a new culture that extends throughout the hotel organization, and between the hotel and its guests, local community, and even its vendors.

6.1 Advantages of Going Greener

6.2 Common environmental challenges and problems in hotels

- Inefficient use of water
- Inefficient use of energy
- Excessive solid waste generation (rubbish, plastics etc)
- No staff participation in environmental schemes
- Poor (or no) monitoring of environmental initiatives

Green hotel strategies in bedrooms

Separate walk-in showers to encourage guests to use the shower instead of the bath, resulting in water saving (many budget hotels do not have bathing facilities, only showers)

Rechargeable batteries for TV remote controls

In-room stationery products produced on recycled paper

No standby lights on TVs

Sensors for utilities/dimmers

Energy Locking System (ELS) on rooms – to reduce electricity consumption when departing from rooms

Create incentives for staff to switch off lights

Master switches in place to control lighting

Provide newspapers only on request to avoid wastage, recycle any spares

Centralised utilities to prevent tampering

Double glazing window insulation and curtains to prevent energy loss

Environmental initiatives within housekeeping, for example, encouraging room customers to re use towels and bed linen a second time

Create signage: 'Switch off lights'

Shower-head flow-reduction design

Flow restrictions on bathroom taps

Purchase energy efficient equipment

Fluorescent light bulbs instead of incandescent

Half-flush facilities on toilet systems

Close off bedroom floors during low periods – fill floors – save electricity

Eco initiatives in the laundry

- Fairtrade cotton to be used wherever possible in linen and uniforms
- Short flushes on washing machines
- Strict specifications for machines – temperatures/water/chemicals
- Old bed linen for dusters or chair slips
- Use chemicals that don't harm the environment
- Eco friendly products/biodegradable
- Investigate using Fairtrade/organic products
- Reduce packaging – bulk amenities, bulk chemicals WRAP
- Use ethical suppliers
- Ensure equipment is maintained and functioning well
- Investigate using solar panels
- Fix leaks promptly

Eco initiatives for public areas

- Hot air blowers in toilets as opposed to paper towels

- Swimming pool covers to prevent heat loss

- Chemical dosage dispensers

- Compact waste so less collections required

- Dedicated recycle area – recycling of paper, plastic, card board, glass, CDs, polythene wrappers, mobile phones, polystyrene, waste cooking oil, toner cartridges and dry cleaning coat hangers

Purchasing energy efficient equipment

Labels to look for when purchasing energy efficient equipment:

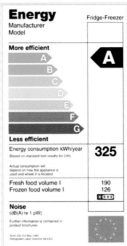

How hotels can achieve good environmental management

- Clear environmental policies and standards
- Employee training
- Employee environmental incentives tied into performance
- Create awareness with employees and customers
- Planned environmental targets
- Accountability and monitor usage
- Environmental benchmarking against other hotel properties
- Have a dedicated environmental group driving forward new initiatives

Tip: don't forget the 3 Rs

Reduce

Reuse

Recycle

6.3 Working with the 'local community'

FOR DISCUSSION

Why is it important for hotels to work with the local community?

Nowadays a very important element for hotels is demonstrating ways in which they can support the local community in which they operate.

Examples of how hotels can work with the local community

- Re-use of furniture and fittings after refurbishments by donating to local charities and businesses

- Donate soap bars to charity

- Provide information on local walks, parks and attractions for guests

- Provide local transport services information to staff and guests

- Use local suppliers

- Employ locals to work in hotels

ACTIVITY 7   20 minutes

Visit the following hotel websites for examples of good practice in hotel environmental management:

http://hiltonworldwide1.hilton.com/en_US/ww/business/environmental.do
http://www.shangri-la.com/en/corporate/aboutus/socialresponsibility
http://www.responsibletravel.com/Accommodation/Accommodation900174.htm

6.4 Hazardous Waste and its Disposal

In a hotel environment, common potential hazardous wastes include:

- Polishes (used on the floor, metal, shoes and furniture).

- Cleaning and disinfecting products (carpet and oven cleaners, detergent, bleach, spot removers and pool chemicals).

- Office products (white-out fluids, permanent ink markers, photocopying and printing fluids).

- Pesticides, fungicides, and herbicides used around the hotel.

- Solvents and aerosols, including air fresheners.

- Oil based paints and varnishes.

- Cooling tower and chilled water chemicals, and freon products.

- Flammables (Sterno gas, lubricating oil).

- Motor oil.

Other hazardous waste can come in the form of solid items, such as batteries, fluorescent lamps, light bulbs, computers and monitors and asbestos.

Take due care with disposal

All hotels are legally responsible for the safe and correct disposal of hazardous waste. Not following proper procedures and regulations can result not only in damage to the environment but also significant fines.

Work with your engineering department to develop a well formulated hazardous waste programme.

Consider what you buy

One way to reduce the amount of waste generated is to scrutinise each product before you buy it, by asking the following:

- Do we really need this product? How much of this product do we actually need?

- Have we checked the product label to see if the product is hazardous? Is there something similar we can use that is less hazardous?

- Do we know how to properly dispose of product containers or the product itself if there is some left over?

- Is there a local collection facility that will accept the unused portion of the product for proper disposal?

Storing hazardous materials

When you have hazardous waste products around, store them in a safe, secure environment until they are disposed of properly.

Storing hazardous waste safely requires careful forethought and planning. Make sure that product labels are attached and readable, and containers are in good condition, and ensure that:

- The area that you are to store the products has an impermeable surface and can be monitored for leaks and spills.

- Products are not in areas open to activities that could damage containers or result in chemical spills.

- The area is not accessible to all staff and the public, and is locked to discourage theft and vandalism.

How to reduce hazardous waste

- Arrange to have unwanted paint removed by contractors, waste removal companies and individual suppliers or distributors.

- Examine office supply catalogues and circulate a recommended list of non toxic office supplies available for purchase.

- Replace acidic drain cleaners with an environmentally friendly enzyme or bacteria cleaning system.

- Look for ways to reduce the entry of hazardous waste materials into your property.

SUMMARY

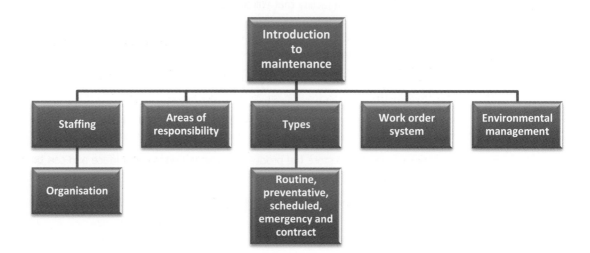

SELF-TEST QUESTIONS

1 Which part of the 'market mix' is well maintained facilities best linked to?

2 How many stages are in the 'product life cycle'?

3 Which employee position is responsible for the management of facilities within the hotel?

4 Which type of hotel would use mainly external contractors to perform maintenance?

5 Name any three strategies to achieve good maintenance within an hotel?

6 What is meant by the abbreviation HVAC?

7 Oiling door hinges, cleaning vents and service checks on electrical equipment are examples of what type of maintenance?

8 A power cut would be an example of what type of maintenance?

9 Which employee would complete a 'work order'?

10 What information would be written when completing a work order request?

SELF-TEST ANSWERS

1 The 'product'.

2 Four stages, introduction, growth, maturity and decline.

3 The Head of Maintenance/Chief Engineer/Maintenance Manager.

4 A budget hotel.

5 Any suitable answer from p. 109.

6 Heating, ventilation and air conditioning.

7 Preventative maintenance.

8 Emergency maintenance.

9 Any employee who needs to report a fault or defect.

10 Name of department, name of employee, date, time, description of problem, urgency.

ANSWERS TO ACTIVITIES

1 Examples include:
- Energy Management System
- Electronic Locking System
- Property Management System
- Point of Sale System

2

What types of maintenance would be required in an in-house laundry?	<ul><li>Checking filters on laundry machines</li><li>Removing lime scale from hot water systems</li><li>Removing lint from dryers</li><li>Lubricating rollers</li></ul>
What is mean by a hotel 'PABX' system?	Private Branch Exchange – a telephone system that facilitates multiple incoming and outgoing telephone calls from one organisation.
List five benefits of an 'electronic locking system' (ELS) for a hotel.	<ul><li>More environmentally friendly</li><li>Safer for customers</li><li>Lost keys pose little risk if found</li><li>Management able to monitor persons using room</li></ul>

BPP LEARNING MEDIA

Detail ten pieces of equipment commonly found in commercial kitchens.	Could include:
	▪ Convection ovens
	▪ Mixers
	▪ Blenders
	▪ Bratt Pans
	▪ Steamers
	▪ Dishwasher
	▪ Walk in freezers
	▪ Griddles
	▪ Grills
	▪ Salamanders
	▪ Microwaves
	▪ Bain maries
	▪ Walk in refrigerators
List ten things that you would need to consider when designing a hotel bedroom.	▪ Visual impact
	▪ Ambience
	▪ Appropriateness for market
	▪ Durability
	▪ Cost
	▪ Access and mobility
	▪ Airflow
	▪ Fire regulations
	▪ Guests with disabilities and the Disability Discrimination Act
	▪ Cleaning and maintenance

3   See the table 'Green hotel strategies in bedrooms' in paragraph 6.2 for some examples.

4

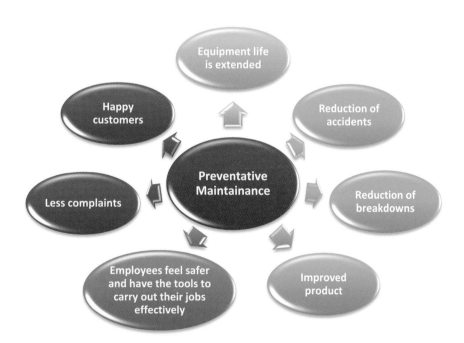

5 One of the main areas to manage is the customers experience ensuring that the building works do not in any way inconvenience their visit which may include noise, smells, facilities not available and building debris.

During this process a housekeeper would communicate with:

- In-house customers
- The Chief Engineer
- Designers
- Architects
- Contractors

6

Bedrooms	Food and Beverage and main kitchen	Leisure club and Spa	Public Areas	External Grounds
■ Leaking taps ■ TV remote control not working	■ Refrigerators not cooling correctly ■ Steamers leaking ■ Fuses broken on equipment ■ Exhaust ducts blocked	■ Jacuzzi filters require cleaning ■ Cracked tiles in pool ■ Sauna's temperature not working correctly	■ Lamp bulbs need replacing ■ Plants needs maintaining ■ Chipped panelling ■ Marks on paintwork	■ Grass cutting ■ Window cleaning ■ Broken fences or gates ■ CCTV cameras require fixing

7 There is no formal answer to this question.

BPP
LEARNING MEDIA

PRACTICE EXAMINATION

This is a real past CTH examination. Once you have completed your studies, you should attempt this under exam conditions. That means allowing yourself the full time available of 2½ hours. Do not look at the suggested answers until you have finished.

QUESTION PRACTICE

CTH diploma courses are all assessed by examination. This method of assessment is used as it is considered to be the fairest method to ensure that students have learnt the things they have been taught.

On the following pages you will find a practice exam for this subject. When you have worked through this study guide and answered the self-test questions you should make a full attempt at the practice exam, preferably under exam conditions. This will give you the opportunity to practise questions in the CTH exam format.

The exam questions in this paper are examples of this subject's questions. The answers provided are notes used by the examiners when marking the exam papers. They are not complete specimen answers but are of the type and style expected. In some cases there is a list of bullet points and in others more text or essay style, however they are representative of the content expected in your responses. Information given contains the main points required by the Chief Examiner.

SECTION 1 – A1 - A10 (2 mark questions)

These questions are looking for factual information and test concise and logical thinking. As a general rule, for a two mark question CTH is looking for one or two word answers or maybe a short sentence. Therefore either text or bullet points will be accepted. If two points are asked for, marks will be allocated for each point. If only one answer is asked for we would expect a short sentence.

Here we are trying to assess your knowledge of the subject and to identify if you can recall the basic principles, methods, techniques and terminology linked to the subject.

SECTION 2 – A11-A15 (4 mark questions)

These questions are looking for factual information and test concise and logical thinking. As a general rule, CTH is looking for bullet points or a short paragraph for the answer to a four mark question. If two or four points are asked for, marks will be allocated for each point. If only one answer is asked for we would expect a few sentences or a short paragraph.

Here we are trying to assess your knowledge of the subject and to identify if you understand and can demonstrate how principles, methods and techniques can be used.

SECTION 3 – B1 (20 mark questions)

These 20 mark questions are looking for factual information and how those facts can be applied to both the subject and the hospitality industry. We expect to see essay style answers to show your knowledge of the subject and its application.

From this section you need to select three questions from a choice of five. **Do not answer more than three as only the first three answers will be marked.** These are essay style questions so you should select the three that you feel you are the most prepared for. No matter how good the answer is, if it does not answer the question you will not be given any marks – marks are only allocated when the answer matches the question.

If you run out of time in the exam jot down the essential points that you intended to include; the examiner will allocate marks for any correct information given.

It is difficult to assess how much you are required to write for a 20 mark question – some people can answer in a page, other people need several pages. What is important is that you answer the question asked – it is about the quality of the answer not the quantity written.

20 mark questions

The following descriptors give you information on the CTH marking scheme and what you need to aim for at each level.

Grade	Explanation
Level 4 **(15-20)**	Demonstrates knowledge of analysis and evaluation of the subject
Level 3 **(11-15)**	Demonstrates knowledge of application of the subject
Level 2 **(6-10)**	Demonstrates knowledge and comprehension of the subject
Level 1 **(1-5)**	Does not demonstrate knowledge and understanding of the subject

Level descriptors

The following level descriptors give you information on what you need to aim for at each grade.

Grade	Explanation
Distinction	Demonstrates knowledge of analysis and evaluation of the subject
Merit	Demonstrates knowledge of application of the subject
Pass	Demonstrates knowledge and comprehension of the subject
Fail	Does not demonstrate knowledge and understanding of the subject

EXAMINATION

CTHCM Diploma in Hotel Management

Subject: **Facilities and Accommodation Operations (DHM 132)**

Series: **January 2008**

Time Allowed: **2.5 hours**

Instructions:

You are allowed **TEN MINUTES** to read through this examination paper before the commencement of the examination. <u>Please read the questions carefully</u>, paying particular attention to the marks allocated to each question or part of a question, and taking account of any special instructions or requirements laid down in any of the questions.

This Examination Paper contains **TWO SECTIONS**.
Answer **ALL** questions in **Section A**.
Answer any **THREE** questions in **Section B**.

On completion of your examination:

Make sure that your name, CTHCM membership number, and centre number are clearly marked at the top of each answer sheet and on any other material you hand in.

Marks Allocation

Section A =   40% of the module grade
Section B =   60% of the module grade

SECTION A

*Answer **all** questions in this section. This section carries a total of **40** marks.*

A1.	Explain what an inventory is used for.	*(2 marks)*
A2.	State two wall coverings for a bathroom.	*(2 marks)*
A3.	Explain what is meant by the term room move.	*(2 marks)*
A4.	When is a bed board used?	*(2 marks)*
A5.	Explain what is meant by the term tog rating.	*(2 marks)*
A6.	List two methods by which the facilities department can reduce utility costs in guest rooms.	*(2 marks)*
A7.	What does the term COSHH mean?	*(2 marks)*
A8.	Describe what is meant by the term day let.	*(2 marks)*
A9.	List two possible uses for a back pack vacuum cleaner.	*(2 marks)*
A10.	List two subjects that are discussed during induction training.	*(2 marks)*
A11.	Explain the term VIP. Who may be given VIP status? Give two examples.	*(4 marks)*
A12.	What is meant by discarded linen? Give two examples of what it can be used for.	*(4 marks)*

A13.
   a) Explain the term Turn Down Service.
   b) State three tasks, which should be carried out during this procedure
      besides the actual turning down of the bed.   *(4 marks)*

A14.   A Housekeeper should always be aware of signs of damp. List four signs
       of damp that can be seen.   *(4 marks)*

A15.   During the course of a day the Housekeeper is likely to come across several
       items that need to be repaired. List four urgent jobs that should be
       reported to the Engineering Department.   *(4 marks)*

SECTION B

*Answer any **3** questions in this section. Each question carries a total of **20** marks.*

B1.
a) Draw a diagram in your answer booklet detailing a typical
   Housekeeping Department organisation chart for a large hotel.   *(10 marks)*

b) Choose four staff positions and describe their main responsibilities.   *(10 marks)*

B2.
Bedding, carpets, furnishings such as curtains and cushions, and uniforms
are made from textiles. Textiles are made from either natural or artificial
fibres or a combination of both.

a) Name two natural fibres and two man-made fibres and give
   examples of their uses.   *(10 marks)*

b) Describe five ways in which hotel linen and its appearance can be
   damaged.   *(10 marks)*

B3.
Devise a checklist summarising the practical methods of reducing
housekeeping costs, showing a minimum of twenty methods of saving.

(20 marks)

B4.
You are employed as the facilities manager of a large city centre hotel and
you have been asked to prepare a list of potential safety and security
hazards in the hotel. Provide a list of at least ten different points with
suggestions to correct any potential dangers.   *(20 marks)*

B5.

a) Draw a diagram in your answer booklet to show the lines of communication in a hotel between the housekeeping department and the other departments. (4 marks)

b) During the course of their work the housekeeper comes into contact with staff responsible for other departments. For smooth running there must be close interdepartmental co-operation. Name four of these departments and in each case state with examples why co-operation is necessary. (16 marks)

PRACTICE EXAMINATION
ANSWERS

SECTION A

A1   An Inventory is a list of goods and materials, or those goods and materials themselves, held available in stock by a business.

A2   Marble, ceramic tiles, mirrors, paint etc

A3   When a guest decides to change room and for any of the following reasons:

- a fault in the room which requires the guest to move out in order to repair it

- the guest wants to extend his stay but the room has been booked for another arriving guest

- the guest wants to stay on a higher/lower floor or in a room with a different aspect

A4   When a guest requires a firm bed or the mattress is beginning to sag.

A5   Duvets are given a tog rating which measures the insulation provided by the quilt. The higher the tog value the greater the insulation.

A6   Electronic key cards that control electricity usage on entering and exiting room,

- dual taps
- towel recycling incentive
- 'don't waste water' signs

Switching off lights when not in use.

A7   Control of substances hazardous to health

A8   When a room is let for part of a day. It may be used as an interview room or for some other business use. It may also be used by a guest who wants to just sleep or rest for a few hours after or before a long journey. The room should be cleaned as quickly as possible when the guest checks out which means it may be re-let again that night.

A9   Cleaning dust from high ceilings, ledges and curtains. Also to remove cobwebs. Vacuuming walls eg fabric and panelling. Cleaning stairs, staircases.

A10 Any of the following: personal hygiene and appearance regulations, courtesy, security, health and safety, fire training, hotel mission and principles, location of the canteen, cloakrooms, linen room, various offices, stores etc.

A11 'Very Important Persons' are usually noted on a special list from Reception. VIPs receive special service. They are often given complimentary fruit, flowers or champagne/drinks in their room or extra giveaways from housekeeping e.g. perfume, special soaps etc. Their rooms must be cleaned and prepared to the highest standards possible.

VIP status may be employees from the hotel's own company e.g. visiting general manager/vice-president or a member of the Royal Family, Head of State, Member of Parliament, Film or Pop Star, T.V. personality or the head of an important company which brings a lot of business to the hotel. And, regular guests.

A12 Discards are condemned articles in the linen room which may be renovated for other uses, for example rags for cleaning, chefs' neck ties, tray clothes, serviettes, drinks coasters, cot sheets, under slips, dust sheets.

A13 a) Turn down service is the term applied to the work maids do, each evening, in guests' bedrooms in hotels.

b) Tasks include: drawing curtains, placing night attire on the bed, switching on bedside lights, emptying waste bins and ashtrays, general tidy of the room, replacing wet or soiled towels, cleaning of bath, wash hand basins and toilet, replacing stationery items, tidying of clothes and pairing of shoes.

A14 A damp room or corridor has a distinctive musty and slightly sour smell, peeling and discoloured wall paper, crumbling plaster, soft rotting wood, peeling paint or emulsion, lifting of tiles, mould on any surface, obvious wet patches.

A15 Blocked or broken toilet, blocked wash hand basin, leaks, fused emergency lights, loose bathroom grab rails, broken mirrors or glass, broken furniture, faulty plugs or wiring. An out of order lift, broken locks. Out of order mini bars/fridge; air conditioning; shower; TV; etc. Broken bed, no hot water.

SECTION B

B1

a)

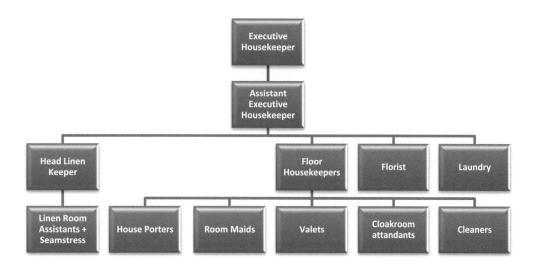

b) The Executive Housekeeper is responsible for the operation of all housekeeping functions in guest rooms, hotel offices, public spaces – including corridors and stairwells and for establishing and maintaining housekeeping standards.

The Assistant Executive Housekeeper aids the Executive Housekeeper in the smooth running of the hotel and relieves him or her on days off. They may also have specific responsibilities e.g. staff training, ordering of stores, and responsibility for the housemen.

The Head Linen Keeper is responsible for the control, supply and repair of the linen, bedding, curtains and any other soft furnishings that may be kept in the Linen Room. The Assistants are responsible for dispatching dirty linen to the laundry and checking the quantities of clean linen when it is returned. If there is not a linen chute then they will collect dirty linen from the guest floors and return clean into the linen cupboards. Seamstresses are responsible for any sewing work that needs to be done throughout the hotel. This includes repairs to linen, bedding, soft furnishings and uniforms, 'remakes' – e.g. making serviettes from discarded tablecloths. They will also carry out alterations to staff uniforms and in some establishments to guest clothes.

Floor Housekeepers supervise the maids, house porters and valets and carry out work delegated by the Executive and Assistant Executive Housekeepers. They are responsible for the standard of cleanliness and appearance of the rooms in their area, and report damage.

Room Maids are responsible for the servicing of the guests' bedrooms, sitting rooms and are on call for service to guests. They may also be asked to clean corridors and service areas and train new maids. Evening Maids are responsible for providing turning down service and answering guest requests e.g. for hot water bottles, extra towels.

House Porters are involved with heavier jobs e.g. moving furniture, clearing away rubbish, high level dusting, turning mattresses, delivering cots/extra beds/bed boards to guest rooms, replenishing stores, shampooing carpets, floor maintenance, vacuuming corridors and staircases.

Cleaners are responsible for cleaning various areas of a hotel e.g. public spaces – toilets, foyers and lounges, sometimes restaurants and bars, back of house areas, locker rooms for staff and offices. They may also be asked to service a section of rooms or vacuum corridors and staircases.

Valet work includes pressing and minor repairs to guest clothes, shoe cleaning, room moves, unpacking and packing for guests.

Cloakroom Attendants are responsible for guarding non-resident guest belongings and attending to the requirements of guests. Also, for keeping the cloakroom clean, neat and tidy.

Florists are responsible for the flower displays and plants in guest rooms, corridor and public areas. They may also arrange flowers for guests and provide bouquets etc. In larger hotels the Head Florist would also oversee the gardeners.

B2

a) Cotton, linen, silk, wool
    Rayon, nylon, polyester, acrylics

    Cotton – bed linen, towels, curtains, table linen, also used in upholstery and clothing
    Linen – bed linen, table linen, hand towels, tea and glass cloths, towels and curtaining
    Silk – wall coverings, cushion covers, sometimes sheets and curtains
    Wool – carpets, upholstery, blankets, clothing

    +

    Rayon – clothing and furnishing fabrics
    Nylon – some bed linen, clothing
    Polyester – clothing, furnishings, bed linen, fillings of cushions & duvets, net curtains
    Acrylics – blankets, carpets, clothing

b) Misuse of linen by waiters and maids and guests
    Carelessness in stripping beds, resulting in sheets getting torn
    Unnecessary use of bleach at the laundry
    Insufficient care of damp and stained linen, resulting in mildew and the spread of ironmould
    Lack of adequate protection during storage, resulting in the folds becoming
    marked and the need for extra laundering
    Insufficient stock and poor rotation, resulting in linen not resting between laundering and the next use
    Careless handling, resulting in soiling, creasing etc.
    Damaged by machinery, linen chute or linen trolleys

B3

Areas where efficiency may be increased	Method of saving
Purchasing	Bulk purchase
	Multi-purpose cleaning agents
	Market research
	Purchase of labour saving devices
	Product analysis and performance testing
Stock Control	Good storekeeping
	Good security systems
	Fire precautions and insurance policies
	Consumption analysis
Staff	Selective interviews
	Induction and training
	Efficient rotas and use of staff
	Work-study and productivity controls
	Reduce manning levels
	Labour saving equipment
	Contract services

Areas where efficiency may be increased	Method of saving
Extravagance	Save it campaign
	Use of computers
	Avoid waste
	Staff training and communication
	Selling off old stock
	Using old pieces of equipment to repair others
	Assess customer and staff needs
	Study financial reports & statistics
	Obtain regular price quotations and prepare comparison studies
	Staff/user suggestion schemes
	Recycling
	Awards and bonus schemes
Housekeeping work load	Use modern equipment
	Use up to date working methods and materials
	Easy to clean surfaces and fabrics
	Reduce or mechanise guest services/supplies
	Fewer giveaways

B4

- Uneven floor
- Signs damaged
- Accumulated rubbish
- Fire doors blocked
- Missing fire apparatus
- Damaged locks in windows and doors
- Lack of safety guards on machinery
- Incorrect protective clothing
- Incorrect storage of chemicals
- Incorrect use of chemicals/cleaning agents

Suggestions to correct any potential dangers

- Properly store and dispose of all materials that may be fire hazards, including cleaning fluids, photocopier inks, and oily or solvent-soaked rags

- Keeping areas clean and tidy will reduce the likelihood of accidents

- Walkways and corridors should never be obstructed

- All spillages should be cleaned up immediately

- Floors and any other flooring surfaces such as tiles and carpet should be kept clean and in good condition

- Dispose of matches, ashes and cigarette ends in proper receptacles

- Never overload circuits

- On stairways, use handrails and take one step at a time. Report worn treads and broken or loose stairs to a Manager/Supervisor. There should be hand railings on all balustrades, slopes and stairs

- Use as much light as you need to get a job done safely and correctly

- Report dusty or out of order lights promptly

- Follow maintenance instructions and report wear and defects

- Be sure guards are always in place before using dangerous equipment

- Safety signs must be kept in good condition and be displayed in a suitable position where they can be easily seen

- Use equipment designed with safe use in mind

- Get help with heavy loads and have one person give signals to lift and put down loads; in addition establish load levels. Teamwork is required when stacking.

- Appoint safety representatives together with a safety committee to review the measures taken to ensure the health and safety at work of employees

- Carry out regular inspections of a building taking notes of any faults, report findings and follow-up – check escape routes are kept clear, alarms function and equipment works

- Produce a Health & Safety check list for Managers/Supervisor to complete

- Incorporate Health & Safety training into both Induction Training and Departmental Training – thereby training staff to work safely, to spot and deal with hazards

- Hold regular fire training sessions together with full staff evacuation of the building

- Discuss Health & Safety issues at staff meetings – make them an agenda point

- Besides providing First Aid facilities – which are a legal requirement, provide personal protective clothing and machine guards

- Design safe systems of work and ensure a planned preventative maintenance system is applied

- Floors should be constructed and maintained to prevent slipping and falling

- Suitable provisions should be made for the cleaning of windows and skylights. Necessary precautions should be taken to prevent persons falling from a window

- Workstations should be designed to be safe and comfortable, e.g. controls should be within easy reach. A suitable seat and footrest must be provided if the task can be accomplished seated.

- Carry out risk assessments in all departments

B5

a) General Manager – Food and Beverage Department – Reception – Reservations – Banqueting - Hall Porters – Maintenance Department – Laundry – Sales – Accounts – Purchasing – Personnel and Training – Security.

b) Reception – besides the cleaning and exchange of uniforms which applies to this and other departments, the housekeeper should notify the receptionists of 'ready rooms' as soon as possible so that rooms are ready for arriving guests and also when rooms are to be 'taken off' for spring cleaning, redecoration and maintenance problems and again when they can be 'put on'. The housekeeper relies on the receptionists to let her know when VIPs are expected, rooms needed on priority to return, room moves and extra departures. Reception may often receive complaints, which then have to be communicated to housekeeping.

Reservations – occupancy, group bookings, planning re-dec etc.

Maintenance – during the course of the day the housekeeper finds many items requiring attention and these faults should be reported as early in the day as possible. If a good relationship exists between the two departments, an urgent repair will be dealt with quickly and not just added to wait its turn on the list. Maintenance is required in other departments besides housekeeping, therefore co-operation is most important. Also, constant liaising over renovation programmes, care of equipment and budgets.

Food and Beverage – co-operation is mainly concerned with linen and there needs to be sufficient well maintained stock to meet demands of the restaurants. The restaurant manager should ensure that the times for exchange of linen are respected and that linen is not mis-used. The housekeeper may be asked to provide carpet spotting or shampooing of these areas and supervise the cleaning to ensure it is done to the desired standard and at convenient times. Room Service waiter should not cause friction with the floor staff, by collecting trays from the rooms in a timely fashion, or by causing careless spills on carpets. Flower displays may be the responsibility of housekeeping and the food and beverage staff may have to inform housekeeping if flowers and plants need attention.

Kitchen – the same co-operation is necessary regarding linen as for the restaurant, also over staff welfare e.g. food as complaints may be discussed on a friendlier basis.

Accounts – many records that the housekeeper keeps will be used by the accounts department, including accurate staff records for payment of wages, budget preparation, inventories also payment of invoices.

Hall Porter – prompt removal of luggage from vacated guest rooms, willingness to loan staff when house porters or valets are not available. Night porters often have to supply articles for guest requests e.g. additional soap, towels, blankets, which the housekeeper provides.

Security – prevention of fire and theft, safe keeping of keys and lost property, also selection of trustworthy staff, control of stores and equipment. Training of staff so that they lock up where necessary and reporting of any suspicious people or circumstances.

Purchasing – discussions between the two departments over suitability versus costs of many items, approval of products before ordering, notification by the housekeeper if articles are to be changed. The housekeeper must keep purchasing well informed of the department's needs so that supplies do not run out.

Laundry (where on premises) – fast and timely turn around of linen and staff uniforms is needed and to a good standard.

Sales – all hotel staff are sales staff since they are all dealing with guests; their appearance, attitude and behaviour will all make an impression on the guests.

Personnel and Training – the housekeeping manager will liaise over interviews and selection of staff, health and safety matters, staff accommodation and training of the housekeeping staff.

Banqueting – linen requirements, cleaning, spring cleaning, floral decorations, uniforms.

BIBLIOGRAPHY

BIBLIOGRAPHY

Casado, MA (2000), *Housekeeping Management*, John Wiley: Canada.

Jones, TJA (2007), *Professional Management of Housekeeping Operations* (5th edition), John Wiley: Canada.

Kappa, MN, Nitschke, A and Schappert, P B (1997), *Managing Housekeeping Operations*, 2nd edn., AHLA: Michigan.

Raghubalan, G and Raghubalan S (2007), *Hotel Housekeeping*, Oxford University Press: New Delhi.

Stipanuk, DM and Roffmann, H (1996), *Facilities Management*, AHLA: Michigan.

Woods, RH and King, JZ (2002), *Leadership and Management in the Hospitality Industry,* AHLA: Michigan.

http://www.macdonaldhotels.co.uk/roxburghe/privacypolicy.htm

INDEX